RYA Advanced Powerboat Handbook

Paul Glatzel

© RYA/Paul Glatzel
First published 2014
Reprinted March 2017, April 2018, March 2019, May 2020, June 2021, April 2022, May 2023, September 2024

The Royal Yachting Association
RYA House, Ensign Way,
Hamble, Southampton,
Hampshire SO31 4YA
Tel: 02380 604 100
E-mail: publications@rya.org.uk
Web: www.rya.org.uk

We welcome feedback on our publications at publications@rya.org.uk

You can check content updates for RYA publications at www.rya.org.uk/go/bookschangelog

ISBN: 978-1-906435981
RYA Order Code: G108

All rights reserved. No part of this publication may be reproduced, stored in a retrieval system, or transmitted, in any form or by any means, electronic, mechanical, photocopying, recording or otherwise, without prior permission in writing from the publishers.

A CIP record of this book is available from the British Library.

Note: While all reasonable care has been taken in the preparation of this book, the publisher takes no responsibility for the use of the methods or products or contracts described in this book.

Cover design and illustrations: Pete Galvin
Typesetting and design: Velveo Design
Proofreading and indexing: Alan Thatcher
Photographic credits: Cheetah Catamarans, Paul Glatzel, Poole Sea Safari, Scorpion RIBs, Solent RIB Charter

Printed in the UK

Foreword

This book is a great addition to any powerboater's library. It takes you forward from the intermediate-level RYA Powerboat Handbook and is focussed on powerboating at a professional level. The official companion to the RYA Advanced Powerboat Course and the RYA Advanced Powerboat Certificate of Competence, it demystifies the more complicated techniques for operating an open vessel by day and night.

Author Paul Glatzel writes in plain English, and the graphics and worked examples bring the concepts to life. Of particular note is the section on navigation. The methods are adapted to what is realistically achievable in an open powerboat with some top tips and practical application of theoretical knowledge. The chapters on wave theory and handling in rougher water go into detail about how to read the conditions and make safe routeing decisions in this dynamic environment.

Whether you're taking friends and family out for fun, or hoping to progress your skills towards the RYA Advanced Powerboat Certificate of Competence, there are plenty of hints and tips to improve your boating.

Rachel Andrews
RYA Chief Instructor, Power

Acknowledgements

Cheetah Catamarans, Commercial RIB Charter, Crest Publications, Nye Davies, Delta RIBs, Paul Glatzel, Icom UK, Glen Mallen, MDL Cobbs Quay Marina, Met Office, Ocean Safety, Poole Sea Safari, Raymarine, RNLI, Paul Sargent, Scorpion RIBs, Solent RIB Charter.

Contains public sector information licensed under the Open Government Licence v3.0 from the United Kingdom Hydrographic Office.

Almanac extract on page 72 courtesy of Imray, Laurie, Norie, and Wilson Ltd.

Further Reading

Other books that merit reading in conjunction with this one include:

RYA Powerboat Handbook (G13/E-G13) – Paul Glatzel

RYA Start Powerboating (G48/E-G48) – Jon Mendez

RYA Navigation Handbook (G6/E-G6) – Melanie Bartlett

RYA Weather Handbook (G133/E-G133) – Chris Tibbs

RYA International Regulations for Preventing Collisions at Sea (G2/E-G2) – Melanie Bartlett

RYA An Introduction to Radar (G34/E-G34) – Melanie Bartlett

RYA Commercial Regulations for Small Vessels (E-G105) – Simon Jinks

These books are available from the RYA webshop (www.rya.org.uk/shop).

Contents

Foreword		2
Acknowledgements		3
Introduction		5
1	**The Role of the Skipper**	6
2	**Working Commercially – Regulations and Qualifications**	8
3	**Types of Craft, Layout and Licensing Requirements**	10
4	**Care and Maintenance**	19
5	**Boat Handling**	21
6	**Collision Regulations**	36
7	**Navigation**	48
8	**Radar and AIS**	78
9	**Weather**	82
10	**Emergency Situations and Man Overboard**	88
11	**Lifesaving Equipment**	93
12	**Searching and Search Patterns**	95
13	**Rescue by Helicopter**	102
14	**Buoyancy and Stability**	107
15	**Wave Theory**	110
16	**Handling in Rougher Water**	115
17	**Higher-Speed Handling**	125
18	**Transfers between Moving Craft**	129
19	**Towing**	131
20	**Cruising**	134
Glossary		136
Index		139

Introduction

The RYA Advanced Powerboat Handbook is aimed at those already working commercially, those working towards being a commercial skipper and leisure users keen to operate at an advanced level.

This handbook supports the RYA Advanced Powerboat course but is equally relevant to those who are simply keen to develop and consolidate their knowledge.

Rather than repeat in depth subjects that have already been covered in either the RYA Powerboat Handbook or in RYA Start Powerboating, some chapters in this book will refer the reader to sections in those titles.

In some areas this handbook addresses subjects in greater detail than is practical or appropriate in the two-day RYA Advanced Powerboat qualification, while some featured aspects are not included in the course. Look out for the flag symbol which indicates this information.

Books and certificates in isolation don't make an individual an advanced powerboater and the challenge for all of us is enhancing and broadening our knowledge in a practical environment afloat. Working alongside capable skippers and learning from them, being aboard various types of craft and boating in different locations all come together to enhance that priceless commodity – experience.

As we seek to push the boundaries of our boating, we should consider a wonderful quote from Mark Twain:

"Twenty years from now you will be more disappointed by the things that you didn't do than by the ones you did do. So throw off the bow lines. Sail away from the safe harbour. Explore, dream, discover."

Have fun boating and enjoy every moment.

Paul Glatzel

Chapter 1

The Role of the Skipper

A great skipper appears relaxed and at ease on a boat. They inspire confidence and share their knowledge to develop those less experienced. They are patient and communicate clearly, and are thorough and precise. They understand their role and their responsibility for the safety of the crew, craft and other water users. They are unlikely to feel the need to shout about their achievements.

Becoming a really effective skipper takes time and effort and requires both a positive attitude and a proactive approach to managing the boat and crew. Some things to try are:

- Spending time afloat with as many skippers on as many craft as possible. Take responsibility for planning and executing entries into unfamiliar locations by day and night under their experienced guidance.
- Creating a training plan detailing the key qualifications you need and ensuring you gain relevant experience. Ensure you allow time for the skills you acquire on courses to bed in. Adopting an approach of 'Undertake course – gain experience – undertake course – gain experience' is very effective.
- Making clear communication key. If your crew don't understand what you want, you probably didn't explain yourself well enough. Choose your words with care. Often, less is more. Create written safety briefs to help you when delivering them to passengers. Written checklists will ensure you follow the operating procedures for the vessel.
- Taking a real interest and pride in the development and progression of those less experienced. Delegate tasks to those best suited to undertake them or to those who will learn most.
- Staying abreast of changes in regulations. Sign up for newsletters from maritime authorities, learn from the analyses of published incidents, attend training courses and updates. Joining a local or national skippers association can be a great way to learn from others' experiences.

A skipper must remember that the sea is a dynamic, changing place and what seemed a safe trip a few hours ago may become unsafe due to changes in weather or crew/boat issues. Be prepared to change plans to ensure safety.

Remember, never delegate responsibility for safety. If things go wrong the skipper is responsible.

Undertaking a Safety Brief

The contents of a safety briefing will vary according to the passage, vessel, crew experience and familiarity of those on board with the safety systems. As a minimum, cover lifejackets, means of issuing distress, fire-fighting equipment and abandonment.

On craft operating at higher speeds, passengers must be properly seated and understand how to deal with the impacts from waves.

Using a checklist makes real sense, even if you have plenty of experience of giving a safety brief.

Chapter 2

Working Commercially – Regulations and Qualifications

Many commercial opportunities exist on fishing boats, wind farm support vessels, safety craft supporting construction projects, helming small, fast craft on charters for corporate events or as crew on a superyacht.

To work commercially you will need to be 'commercially endorsed', which requires you to understand your responsibilities as a skipper and the legislation applying to your role.

There are five main conventions that apply wherever you work:

- IRPCS – International Regulations for Preventing Collisions at Sea
- MARPOL – International Convention for the Prevention of Pollution from Ships
- SOLAS – International Convention for the Safety of Life at Sea
- STCW – International Convention on Standards of Training, Certification and Watchkeeping for Seafarers
- UNCLOS – United Nations Convention on the Law of the Sea

These conventions are produced by the IMO (International Maritime Organisation), which is part of the UN. You should understand how they impact on you and where to learn more if needed.

WORKING COMMERCIALLY – REGULATIONS AND QUALIFICATIONS | 2

Key Aspects

SOLAS Chapter V ('Safety of Navigation'): Passage planning – a plan is needed before going 'to sea'. It should consider weather; tides; the nature of the passage; ports of refuge and any other relevant factors. Responding to distress – where possible, and safe to do so, assist vessels in distress and report navigational hazards. Radar reflectors – these should be carried and fitted where possible. Lifesaving signals – these should also be kept on board and the distress system should not be misused.

IRPCS (The 'ColRegs'): Know the key rules and be aware of the regulations relating to navigation lights, shapes and sound signals as these vary according to the length of vessel and nature of its work.

STCW: Compliance certification may be required when working on craft over 24m or on UK-flagged vessels overseas.

MARPOL: Preventing pollution is common sense. A failure to understand and apply the rules can lead to prosecution/significant fines.

Gaining Commercial Endorsement

To become commercially qualified you will typically follow one of two routes:

- Attach a commercial endorsement to an existing qualification. A certain level of experience will be required.
- Undertake an examination to assess your competence.

Typically, the examined route allows you to go further from a safe haven, possibly by day and night, and in a wider range of conditions.

There are various levels of qualification and examination.

Not all qualifications can be commercially endorsed. Check which can be with your local maritime agency.

You will usually need sea survival, VHF radio and first aid qualifications. A medical is also needed.

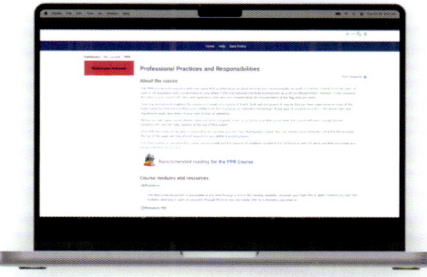

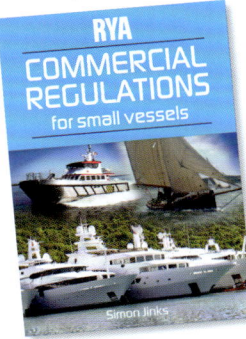

Don't forget that as a commercial skipper you have an ongoing responsibility to stay abreast of changes to the rules and regulations that will affect you, your crew and the vessels that you are qualified to helm.

If you run your own commercial craft then you will have additional responsibilities as an 'Owner/Managing Agent'. However, even as a skipper employed to be in charge of a craft, you will need to understand the requirements for the craft itself.

Chapter 3

Types of Craft, Layout and Licensing Requirements

Many factors influence the type of craft you choose. For commercial operators it will be the location, typical sea and weather conditions, and the nature of the job that needs doing. For leisure users it may purely be a matter of personal preference.

A vessel's seakeeping ability and its suitability to undertake certain tasks or passages will depend on various factors such as hull shape/design, engine type and positioning, and the type of drive system chosen. The ergonomics of the helm position will also significantly impact the ability of the helm to handle their craft in certain conditions and for sustained periods.

If a vessel is to work commercially (even if those on board are not paying to be there) then it will almost certainly need to be certified by a local maritime agency and will need to carry minimum levels of equipment according to its area of operation. The vessel will also need to be regularly inspected.

TYPES OF CRAFT, LAYOUT AND LICENSING REQUIREMENTS 3

Hull Design and Strength

Planing: Allows high-speed operation. Fore–aft strakes create lift; once 'on the plane' the craft runs on surface of the water. Various hull shapes available with 'deep V' most popular. Angle of 'V' determines ability to slice through waves. Flatter hulls 'slam' more.

Catamaran: Common for dive/fishing charter and patrol craft. Good deck area, stability and seakeeping.

Displacement: Low speed but very good seakeeping. Limited use commercially except fishing vessels, tugs etc.

Semi-displacement: Good seakeeping. Combines benefits of displacement craft with greater speed. Often used for patrol and harbour/pilot launches.

Hull strength and rigidity contribute to the seakeeping qualities of the craft. Poorly designed/constructed hulls flex in rougher conditions, possibly leading to stress damage or failure.

RYA ADVANCED POWERBOAT HANDBOOK

3 TYPES OF CRAFT, LAYOUT AND LICENSING REQUIREMENTS

A fine bow with little volume will have less buoyancy than a larger flared bow. Lift created by buoyancy may prevent the bow burying into waves. In contrast, a fine bow will cut better through waves. There is no perfect solution and helms should understand the craft they are handling and the characteristics of the hull. This will be achieved simply by seatime and experience in that craft.

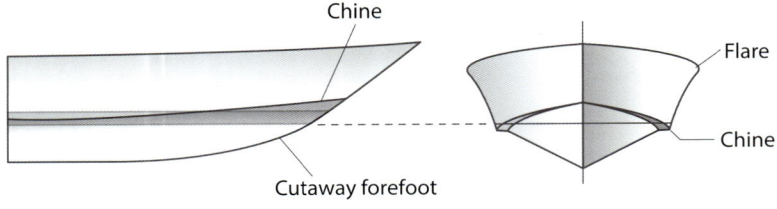

Cutaway forefoot

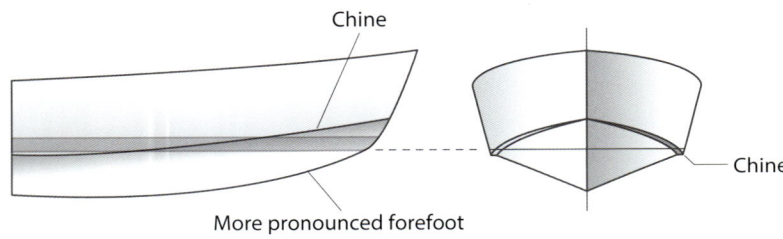

More pronounced forefoot

Engines, Drive and Control Systems

Engines

Single or twin outboards are common in craft up to about 24ft in length. Their performance is good and engines can be changed rapidly. Typically, they are four-stroke and 'high-tech', and their ability to trim high is useful in shallower waters.

Inboards can be petrol or diesel engines, but diesels are always fitted for commercial craft. They are often simpler to maintain than outboards. The engine position moves the craft's centre of gravity forward, influencing handling, and the vessel layout is influenced by the engine position. They can drive through shafts, outdrives or jets.

TYPES OF CRAFT, LAYOUT AND LICENSING REQUIREMENTS 3

Drive Systems

Shaftdrives: Common on smaller 'fast fisher'-type vessels as well as larger craft, they are simple and cheap to maintain. Twin installations are the preferred choice of many commercial skippers.

Outdrives (or 'sterndrives'): Single or twin. Contra-rotating props offer very good slow-speed control. Outdrives are more expensive to maintain than 'shafts'.

Forward-facing drives: Increasingly popular, these are still the preserve of larger craft. They are considered efficient relative to outdrives and are available with joystick control.

Jet drives: Popular for shallow-water operation or where there may be debris or people in the water. Very manoeuvrable – especially twin installations.

Outdrive, shaftdrive and jet arrangements are available as twin or single installations.

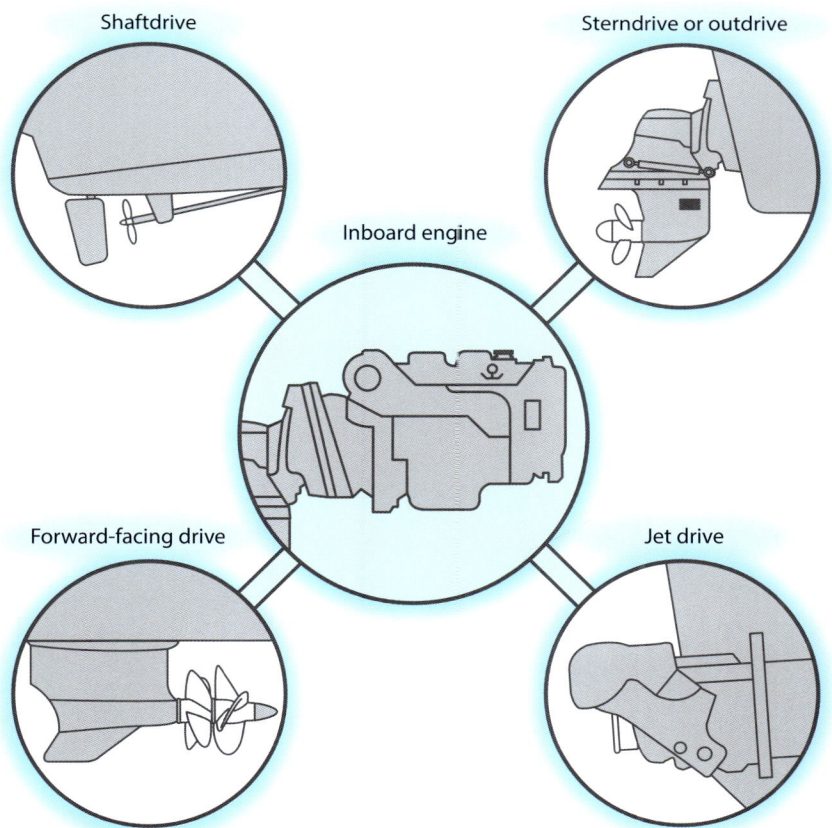

3 TYPES OF CRAFT, LAYOUT AND LICENSING REQUIREMENTS

Control Systems

Throttles directly engage gears through cables or by using electronics. Electronic systems are very smooth but in rougher conditions the lack of physical resistance to movement (versus cable-driven versions) can lead to inadvertent throttle adjustment as the helm's hands are moved by sea conditions. A well-set-up craft will ensure the helm can brace their hand on or near the throttles. Combinations of 'fly by wire' controls and electronic rams to engage gears can make fixing issues afloat more challenging with electronic systems.

Joystick systems integrate engines, steering and thrusters to move the vessel in any direction. They are available twin-engined for forward-facing drives, jets, outboards, outdrives and occasionally shaftdrives.

Enclosed or Open Wheelhouse?

The ability to keep kit dry, have a galley and shelter passengers may all influence the decision of whether or not to have a wheelhouse.

A wheelhouse is essential in colder, wetter locations, but it may reduce the 'feel' the helm has for the surroundings.

A wheelhouse roof provides options for fitting electronics and lifesaving appliances, but beware the impact on stability if heavy items raise the vessel's centre of gravity.

For commercial craft it is usually a licensing requirement that there is an enclosed wheelhouse for night-time operation or in rougher conditions.

Craft Layout

The seats closer to the bow in RIBs experience most vertical movement, increasing impacts on passengers. A rear helm position reduces impacts for the crew, while a forward helm position reduces the crew's ability to see passengers but ensures that the helm 'feels' conditions. In RIBs, passengers' feet should sit level on deck to allow uniform transference of impacts.

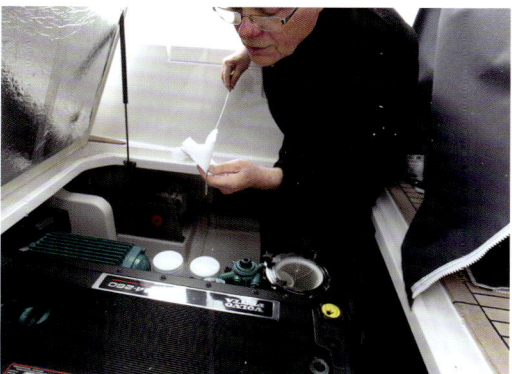

Angles of windows and positions of mullions and doors all influence ability to spot objects and vessels. Blind spots should be minimal in well-designed vessels.

Easy access to engines and the ability to make simple daily checks are essential. Level decks and accessible storage for lifesaving appliances are similarly important.

Operators of craft used at higher speeds need to pay considerable attention to the protection of crew and passengers from impact-related injuries.

3 TYPES OF CRAFT, LAYOUT AND LICENSING REQUIREMENTS

Seating Arrangements and Shock-Mitigation Solutions

It is important to limit/lessen the effect of repetitive wave impacts that lead to fatigue and injury.

In RIBs, 'jockey' seats are generally preferable to bench seats as they reduce the effects of wave impacts by utilising the body's natural 'shock absorbers'. Suspension seats can be very effective and are increasingly common. 'Wrap around' stand-up positions are fitted to some vessels.

Seats positioned forward in a craft may transmit considerable impacts due to the greater vertical movements towards the bow of a vessel.

Decks can be fitted with shock-impact matting or the entire deck area can be 'suspended'. If matting is fitted post-manufacture, ensure the seating and steering positions are not compromised due to effectively raising the deck by 5–10cm.

Footstraps are often fitted in craft operating in rougher conditions or at higher speeds to keep the crews' or passengers' feet in contact with the deck and those on board in their seats.

Seats fitted with suspension systems in cabin boats are very effective but skippers must be careful as others on board may not be protected in the same way. Craft should be driven to protect the most vulnerable person.

Choosing footwear with inbuilt impact protection can also make a real difference.

Whatever methods are used to attempt to mitigate shock impact, the responsibility remains with the helm to drive their craft in a way appropriate to the conditions with due consideration to those on board.

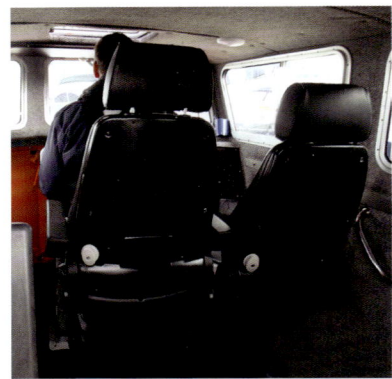

The Ergonomics of the Helm/Navigator Position

The throttle, steering and other key controls should be within easy reach of the helm without them bending or stooping. Position gauges for easy viewing.

Navigation systems should allow the crew to operate but be visible and accessible to the helm. Positioning systems solely for the helm's use should be avoided.

Licensing Requirements

A vessel operating commercially will need to be 'certified' by an authorised body. An operator will need to consider various factors when seeking to certify their vessel:

- The area of operation including day or day & night operation.
- The number of passengers that could be carried.
- The type of vessel – for example, open RIB or an enclosed catamaran.

Area of operation: Countries differ but all typically define varying areas of operation. For example, in the UK the Maritime & Coastguard Agency produces a document which details all of the key facts relating to operating a commercial vessel. It specifies various areas of operation:

- Category 6 – Within three miles of a Nominated Departure Point (NDP) and three miles of land in favourable weather.
- Category 5 – Within 20 miles of an NDP in favourable weather.
- Category 4 – Twenty miles from a safe haven in daylight and favourable weather.
- Category 3 – Twenty miles from a safe haven by day or night.
- Category 2 – Sixty miles from a safe haven by day or night.

A Nominated Departure Point is specific to the vessel and is detailed in its licence.

Vessels such as Police boats and lifeboats will typically have their own set of licensing rules, although they are usually broadly similar to those for 'normal' commercial vessels.

3 | TYPES OF CRAFT, LAYOUT AND LICENSING REQUIREMENTS

The operator will need to ensure that the skipper and crew meet the manning requirements for the vessel.

There will be a list of the required equipment according to the category of operation. For example, the fire-fighting equipment a vessel needs to carry, the water-pumping arrangements, the number of flares and other means of issuing distress will all vary according to the category of operation.

The number of passengers a vessel can carry will appear on the coding licence and will be limited to a maximum of 12. The number of crew will also be detailed. The volume of equipment such as lifejackets and liferafts that need to be carried will vary according to the number of people on board.

A commercial operator will need to produce risk assessments and standard operating procedures to ensure that their vessel is run safely and that the crew members understand their responsibilities. A skipper needs to understand, embrace and apply these assessments and procedures fully.

Chapter 4

Care and Maintenance

Look after a boat and it will look after you. A regular schedule of maintenance coupled to the ability to fault-find and fix routine issues is a key aspect of being a competent skipper.

Create a daily checklist covering all lifesaving equipment, engines and other systems. Regular checks may prevent serious failures at sea.

A skipper should know how to identify and fix the common problems that may occur when afloat. What these are will vary according to the type of craft and the drive system it is fitted with. What you will be able to fix may be very limited on some newer engines.

Common issues when afloat include:

- Loose electrical connections may prevent a vessel from (re)starting.
- Loose belts may slip and cause charging issues or impact in other ways. Know how to tighten the belts before you go afloat as often they are in inaccessible locations.
- Likewise, know how to change belts as sometimes it will require the removal of another belt or component. Practise doing it before you need to do so for real.

- Fuel filters can become blocked. This is especially true on craft not usually used in rougher conditions where sediment can be stirred up in the tank. Often, craft have two types of fuel filter – know how to change them and 're-prime' the fuel system if needed.
- Impellers drive cooling water around an engine. Know how to change them and carry the tools needed to do so.

RYA ADVANCED POWERBOAT HANDBOOK

4 CARE AND MAINTENANCE

 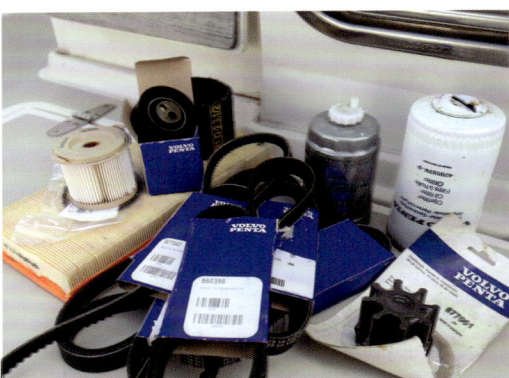

- If you need to, propellers can sometimes be changed or removed when the craft is still in the water. Know how to do so and be careful not to lose any parts. Ensure items such as thrust washers are transferred between props if changing them.

- Carry plenty of spares, especially if operating further offshore or in remote areas. Have the correct tools on board – specialist tools are sometimes needed for certain tasks.

Nothing can replace experience as a way to learn how to deal with engine issues as, over time, most skippers will have to deal with most common problems.

Learning about a particular engine or drive arrangement from those more experienced than you can be invaluable, as they can alert you to the common issues with that setup. Undertaking a course is a good way to improve knowledge, or asking a marine engineer to spend time with you as you change belts and impellers and develop your skills is time well spent.

Develop and follow a maintenance program for the vessel. This will be a requirement for licensed vessels anyway.

Carbon Monoxide

All cooking and heating appliances can produce carbon monoxide if not properly ventilated. Exhaust fumes from machinery may also accumulate in enclosed space, and even in open cockpits if stationary or travelling at low speed.

Carbon monoxide is colourless, odourless, and poisoning can be deadly. The first signs are headaches, tiredness, sickness, and dizziness. It is recommended that you fit a carbon monoxide detector and test it regularly.

To ensure adequate ventilation throughout the cabin, make sure that any ventilators are clear of obstructions.

Chapter 5

Boat Handling

Competent boat handling comes from understanding how the elements affect a boat, how altering steering and engaging gear move a craft, and from plenty of practice. Advanced-level boat handling means being able to helm your vessel in close-quarter situations in any state of wind and stream.

Before looking at some specific manoeuvres with various craft, here is a reminder of some of the key factors affecting boat handling:

Wind

Most craft naturally lie at right angles to the wind or with their bow slightly downwind. The greater the wind or 'windage' on the craft or a heavier stern relative to the bow, the quicker the craft will settle to this position.

Most craft will sit well stern-to-wind holding position using astern.

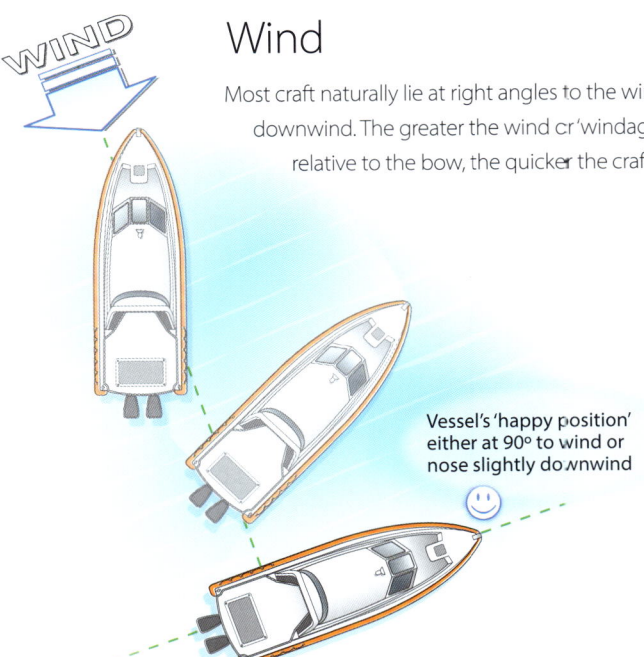

Vessel's 'happy position' either at 90° to wind or nose slightly downwind

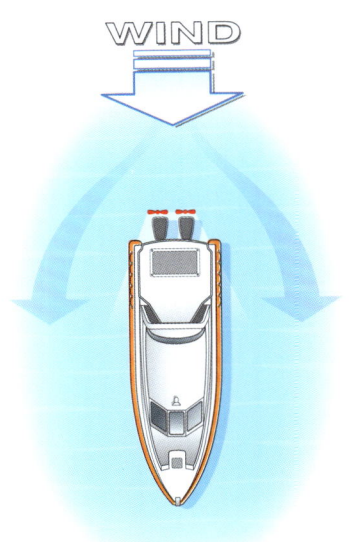

5 BOAT HANDLING

Stream (Tide or Current)

Stream may hinder or assist manoeuvring. Pointing the bow (or stern) into the stream allows water flow past the hull, slowing movement and helping precise handling.

Stream (or wind) allows a vessel to 'ferry glide' sideways.

Angle the craft so the wind/stream creates a sideways force on the vessel. This works too for stern to wind/stream. This allows slow, controlled movement sideways and is a very effective technique to get into some tight berths.

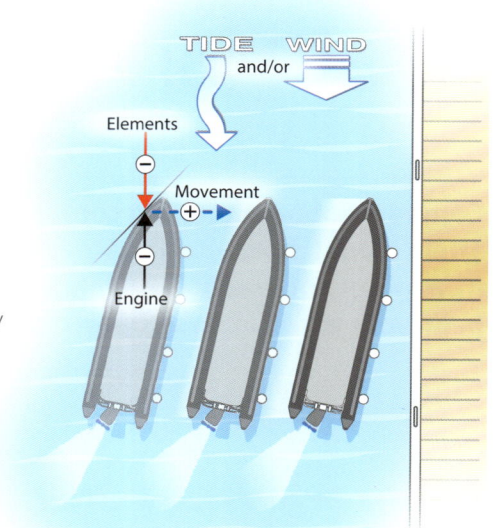

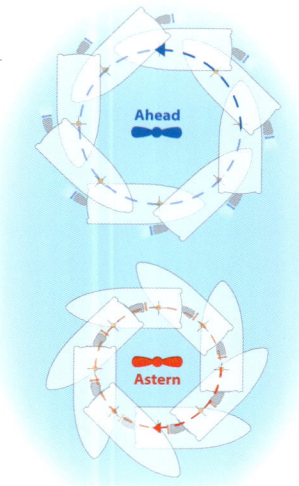

Pivot Points

In forward gear, a craft pivots around a point forward of its centre. When going astern, the pivot point moves aft with the effect of making the turn tighter.

Propwalk

The rotation of propeller creates sideways movement – 'propwalk' (or 'paddlewheel effect'). It is most pronounced when going astern and on shaft-drive vessels, and is almost non-existent with outboards/outdrives.

A propeller rotating clockwise when going ahead ('right-hand prop') drags the stern to port when going astern. Twin shaftdrives maximise the effect, allowing precise boat handling – see page 25.

To determine which way the stern will 'kick' when astern is engaged, when alongside, engage astern – the wash appearing to starboard suggests stern will move to port.

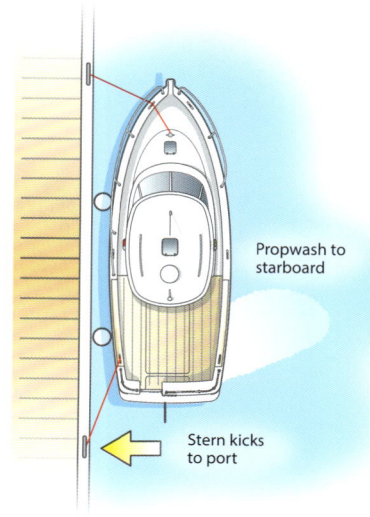

BOAT HANDLING 5

Leverage with Twin Outdrives/Outboards

The offset of the propellers from the centreline of the craft creates a turning effect both ahead and astern.

Using steering as well will increase the rate of turn.

Think of engines as either 'inside' or 'outside' of the turn. When turning, the 'inside' engine will have less effect in contrast to 'outside' engine.

Sometimes, using the engine with 'less' effect on its own may be beneficial.

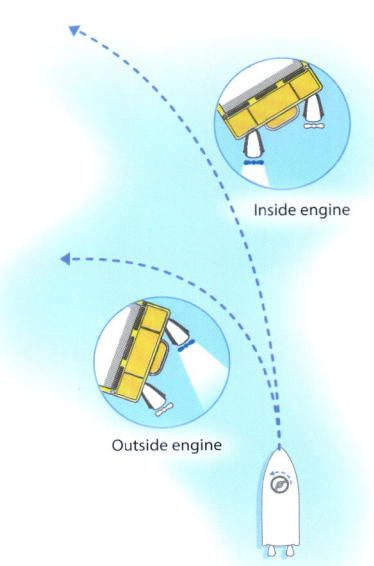

Inside engine

Outside engine

Momentum – Who's in Control?

When handling a craft at slow speed in a close-quarter situation, the helm must balance wind, stream and how the vessel is moving to achieve the desired manoeuvre.

Wind and stream may act to reduce momentum. Be careful to ensure excessive momentum is not added, as this needs removing at some stage. Use the minimum amount to achieve the objective. Too much speed through a marina will also make it difficult to react to other craft or hazards. Go into/out of gear to keep the speed down and consider engaging just one engine on twin-engine craft.

Too little momentum, though, and the wind or stream becomes dominant. This may be the desired effect but the helm must always ensure that they're in charge and not the elements.

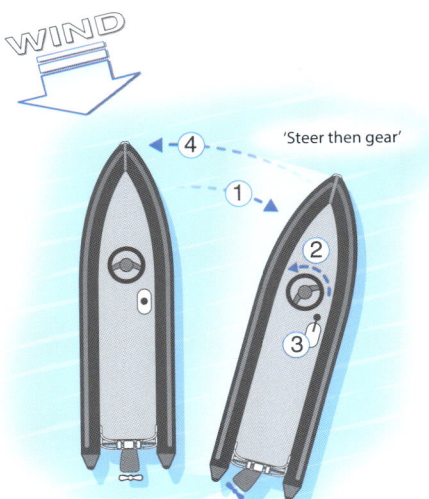

Keeping Bow into Wind

Holding the bow into wind (or just off it) is a key skill, as the ability to control the bow impacts close-quarter manoeuvres. Control the bow by applying steering before engaging gear briefly ('steer then gear'). The same effect can usually be achieved using astern and opposite turn, except for shaftdrives.

RYA ADVANCED POWERBOAT HANDBOOK   23

5 BOAT HANDLING

Handling Outdrive- or Outboard-Powered Craft

Single Engine

'Steer then gear' is taught as the primary technique for outdrive/outboard-powered craft. However, as competence develops, a helm may adopt a more flexible approach. When coming alongside, initially going astern then turning towards the pontoon as much (or as little) as is needed to 'pull' the stern in may be smoother than fully turning in then going astern (i.e. 'gear then steer', or 'gear + steer' as one movement, rather than 'steer then gear').

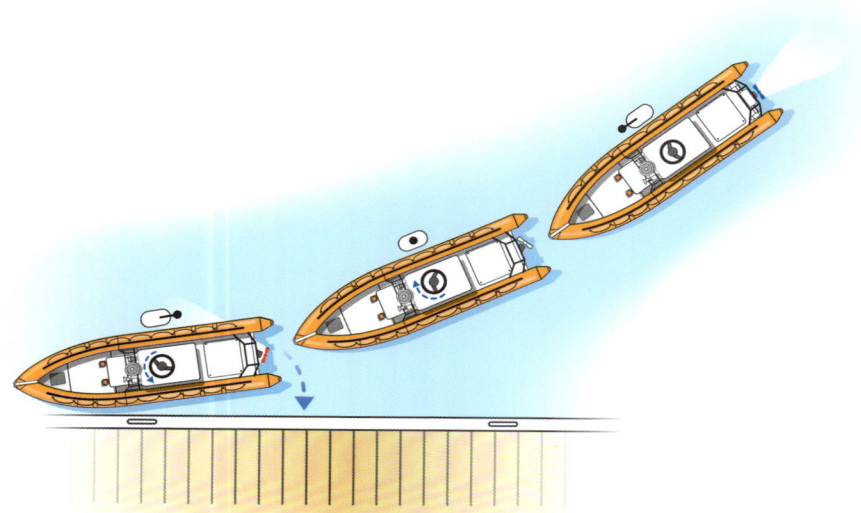

Twin Engines

Twin-engined outdrive- or outboard-powered craft can be handled in various ways:

- By using each engine independently according to which one has the required effect – using the 'steer then gear' technique.
- By centring drives and using the offset of the propellers from the centreline to create turn – in effect treating the vessel as a twin shaftdrive-type installation.
- By using a combination of these techniques.

Which is best is a matter of preference but may be influenced by the craft and the separation between the engines. More separation gives greater leverage.

BOAT HANDLING 5

Some tips:

Craft may move sideways if the 'outside' (or only) engine is alternated between ahead and astern. This will work very effectively with the helm hard over, the outside engine astern and the bow thruster engaged in the direction of travel.

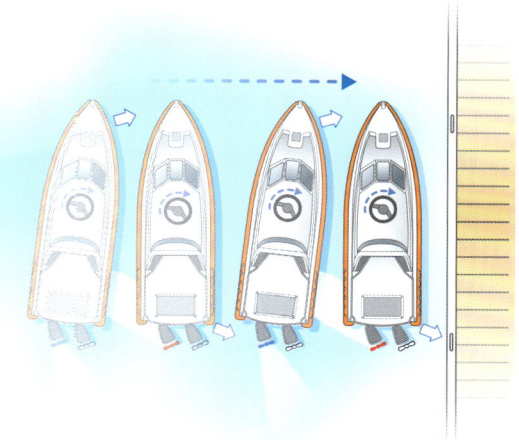

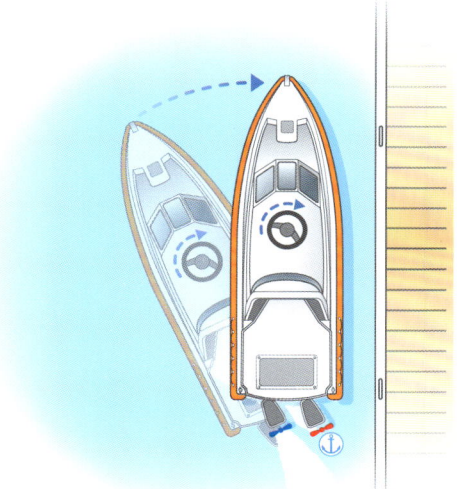

When turning, applying full helm with the engine on the outside of the turn in 'ahead' while the inner engine is astern means that the inner engine holds the position and tightens the turn.

Shaftdrives

Single engines are common and handle well but some craft struggle to steer when going astern. Astern steerage is only available once water is flowing past the rudder. This, when combined with the effect of propwalk, may lead the stern to creep in one direction.

When entering a berth bow first, the stern will kick one way (usually port) when going astern. This may make a 'starboard side to' berth more challenging.

Twin engines tend to be fitted on vessels longer than 30ft and give good handling characteristics.

5 BOAT HANDLING

Usually the starboard engine has a propeller fitted that walks to port when going astern, while the port engine does the opposite – contra-rotation! The combination of propwalk and leverage effect allows tight turns to be made.

Twin shaftdrives turn very well with a combination of throttle and helm. To do so, apply full helm in the direction of the turn, then put one engine ahead and the other astern.

Resist the urge to increase power if a vessel creeps forward (or backwards) while turning. Instead, go to neutral on the forward engine momentarily. Increasing power is usually unnecessary and risks a problem if one engine fails.

Leaving the less-dominant drive in gear (normally astern) and using the other drive into and out of gear can enable very precise position-holding during a turn.

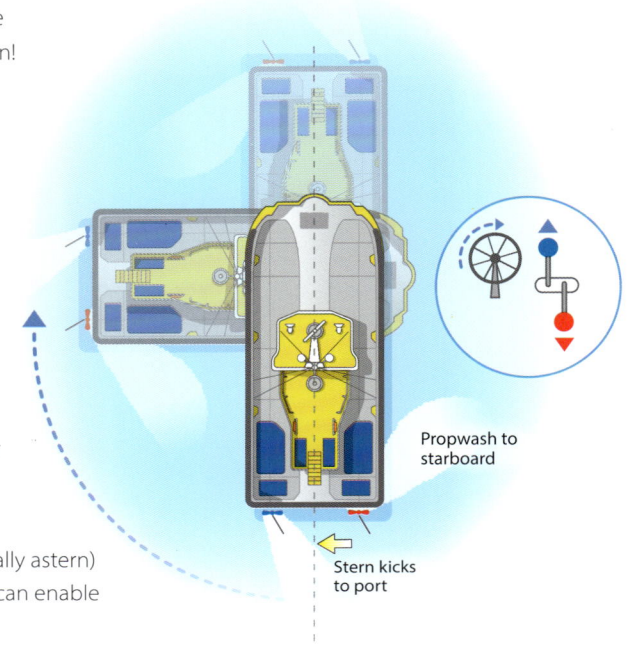

Jet Drives

Jet-drive craft are increasingly popular both in single- and twin-engine form and are highly manoeuvrable. The slow-speed techniques are different to outdrive/outboard and shaftdrive craft.

The engine drives an impeller that forces water through a steerable nozzle.

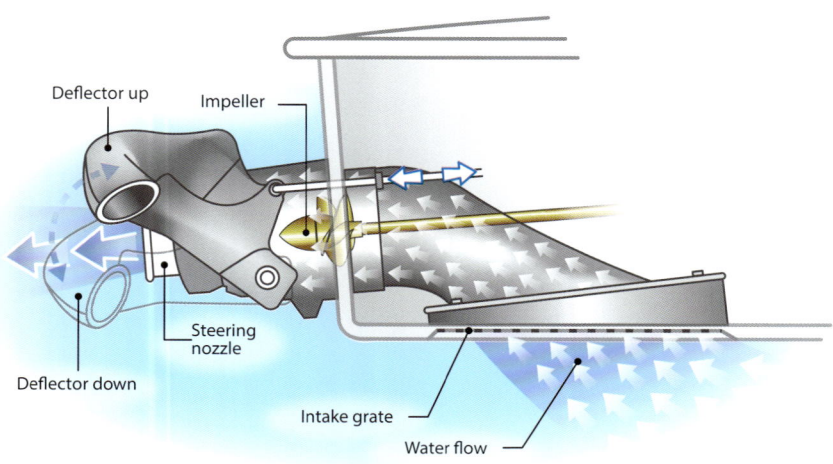

BOAT HANDLING 5

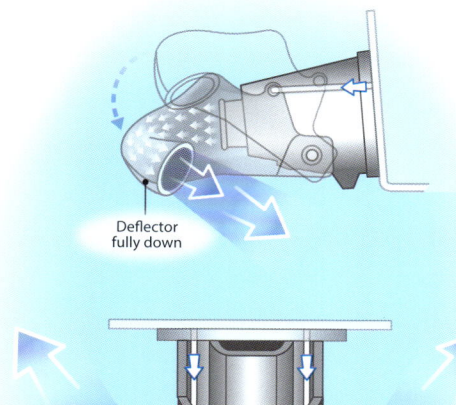

Astern

A deflector (often referred to as the 'bucket') introduced to the jet stream redirects water flow. Vessel moves astern.

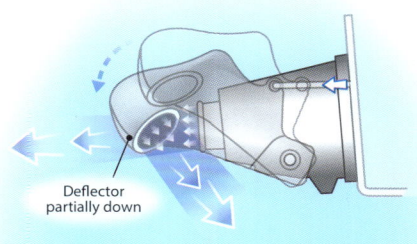

Static

When positioned partially into the flow, the deflector holds the vessel static.

Subtle adjustments to steering may be needed to maintain heading.

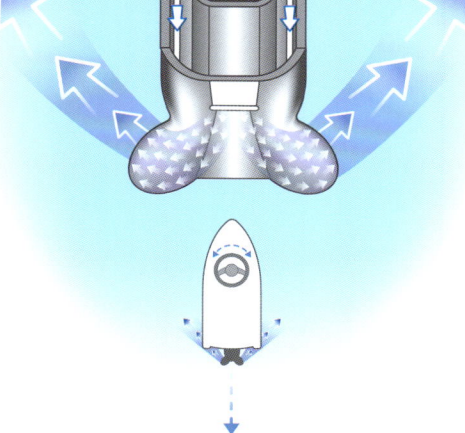

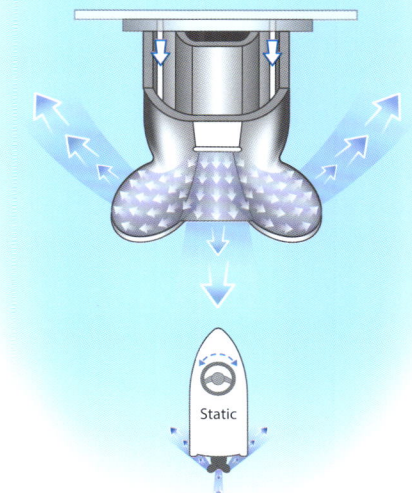

5 BOAT HANDLING

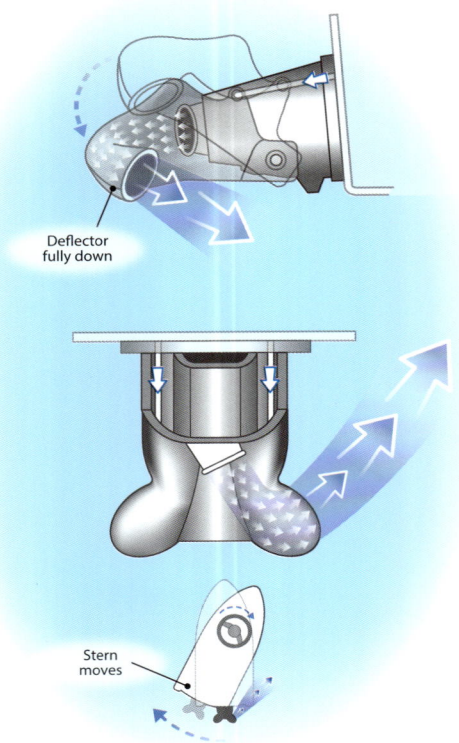

With the deflector down, directing the nozzle to starboard redirects the thrust to starboard, pushing the stern to port.

Moving Sideways – 'Crabbing'

Crabbing is moving the boat sideways without any ahead/astern movement. To crab to port:

- Port deflector fully down
- Starboard deflector in ahead/up position but be ready to adjust constantly to limit forward movement
- Use helm to keep boat on straight heading

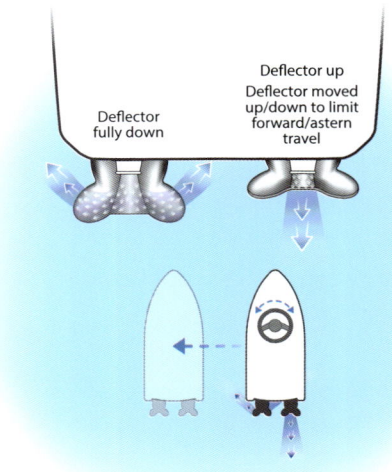

BOAT HANDLING | 5

Forward-facing Drives

These handle similarly to craft with twin-outdrives setup. Optional joystick control allows independent steering of engines, giving movement in all directions.

Joystick Control

Joystick control is also available for twin-outdrive or outboard installations and, on larger vessels, twin shaftdrives.

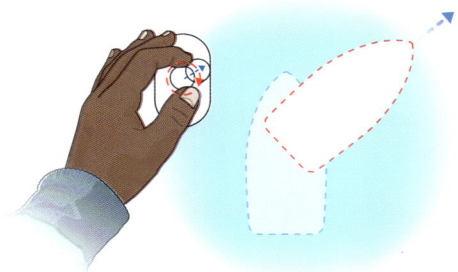

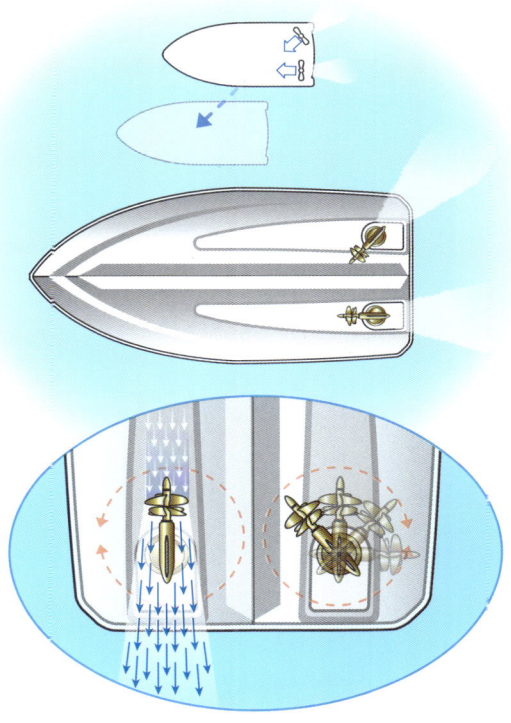

Thrusters

Thrusters are fitted to many craft over about 26ft. They help control the bow (and sometimes the stern). A thruster is there to be used but be careful not to rely on it too much. Treat it as an 'assistant' rather than the main way to achieve a manoeuvre.

Thrusters can place a heavy load on batteries and cables and may overheat if used for too long.

Before approaching a berth, always ensure thrusters are switched on and working in case they are needed.

5 BOAT HANDLING

Manoeuvring in Marinas – Hints and Tips

Constantly assess the wind, the stream and the actions of other vessels. Look for crew tending lines, vessels with engines running and areas where wind and stream may have an increased impact.

When alongside a pontoon, it is generally easier to reverse away as the location of the pivot point and the curve of the bow makes for an easier departure.

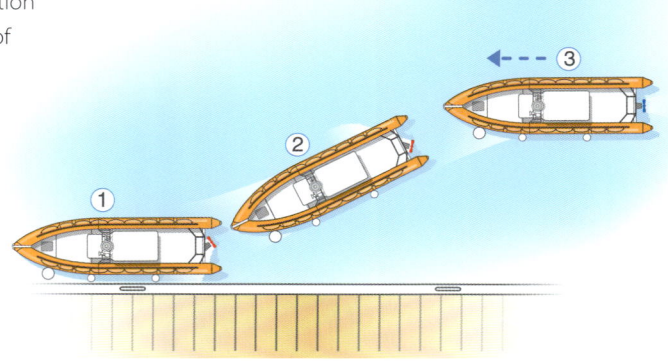

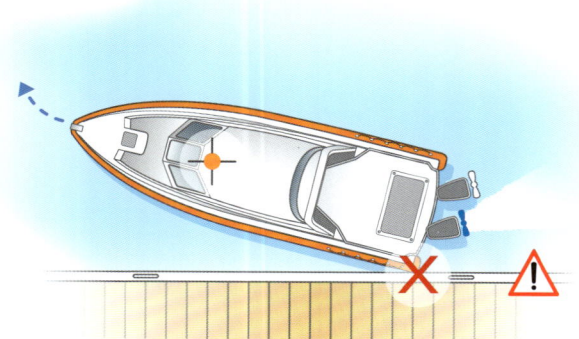

Turning away from a pontoon and going ahead is more difficult due to the pivot point. Damage is more likely.

Using the engine on the inside of the turn of a twin outdrive/outboard in astern when turned away from a pontoon should gently lift the craft away.

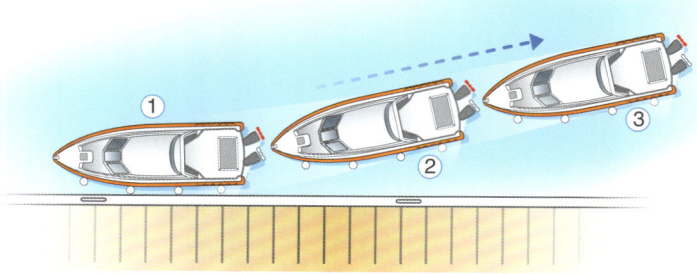

BOAT HANDLING 5

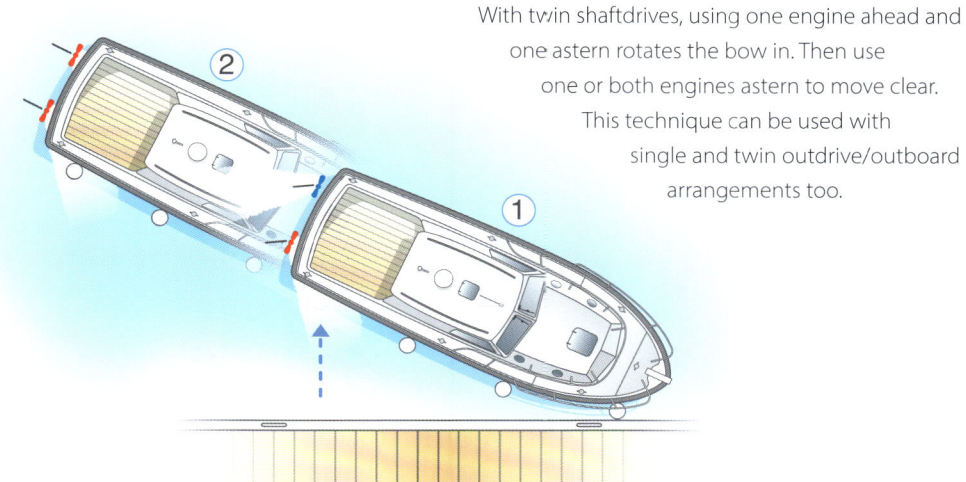

With twin shaftdrives, using one engine ahead and one astern rotates the bow in. Then use one or both engines astern to move clear. This technique can be used with single and twin outdrive/outboard arrangements too.

Using Lines to Assist Leaving and Coming Alongside

A spring preventing rearward movement is rigged at the bow. The line is then slipped and pulled aboard. NEVER use springs with a person holding a line without taking a turn around a cleat. To come alongside, the process is reversed – get bow line on, secure, then reverse and steer stern towards pontoon.

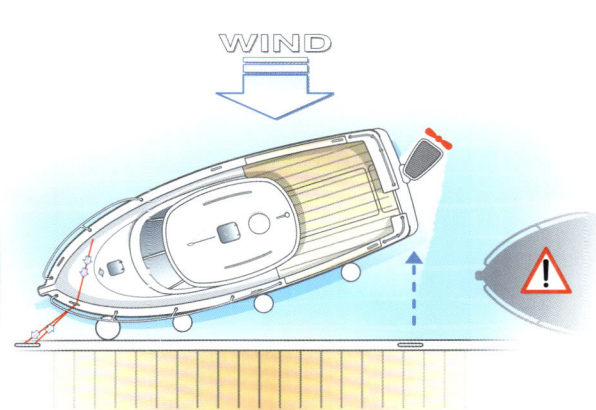

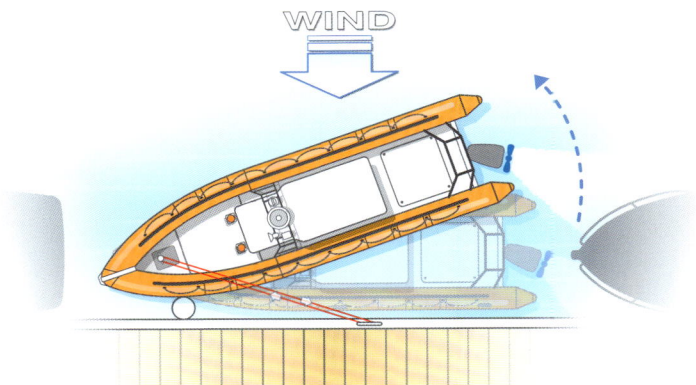

The spring at the bow is rigged to hold the position. Turning towards the pontoon and gently engaging ahead pushes the stern out. Go to neutral, cast off when clear, and reverse out.

RYA ADVANCED POWERBOAT HANDBOOK

5 BOAT HANDLING

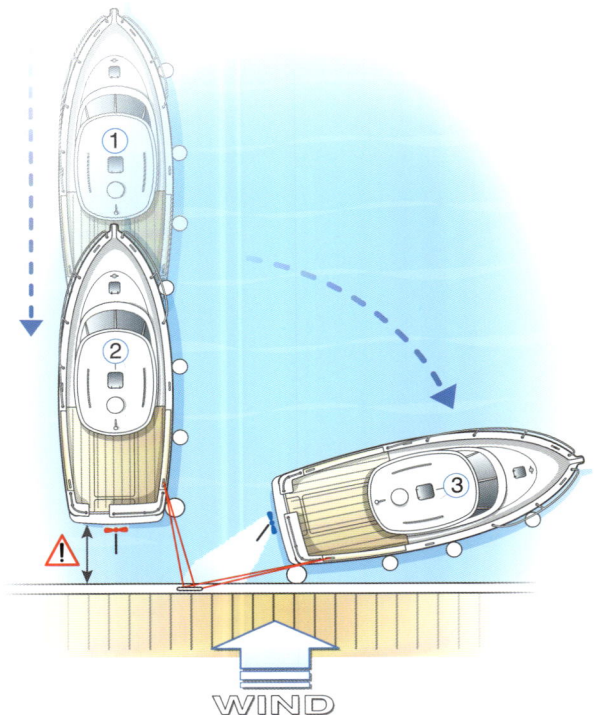

Craft hold very well stern-to-wind and often the stern is the most accessible area for crew. Reverse towards a cleat, lasso and secure. Turn towards the pontoon – engaging ahead brings the bow in.

Other Techniques

In a marina, ensure you have as much room to escape as possible. Be mid-channel or on the upwind side if being blown towards other craft, unless another craft is ahead.

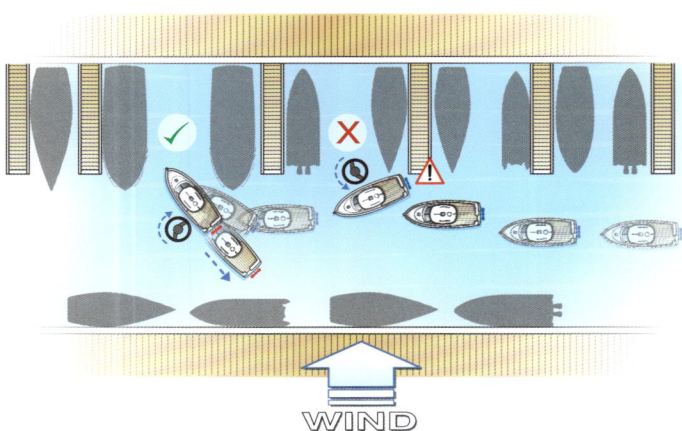

If 'pushed' towards the other craft by wind, turning away may cause impact. Briefly turn towards the craft to push stern away, and reverse out positively.

Approaching Berths

Often, positioning the craft so it is approaching a berth with an 'open' face and momentum carrying it is easiest.

In this example, turning to port and going astern arrests momentum and starts the turn, in contrast to turning to starboard and engaging ahead. This may speed up the craft, which 'slides' away faster downwind.

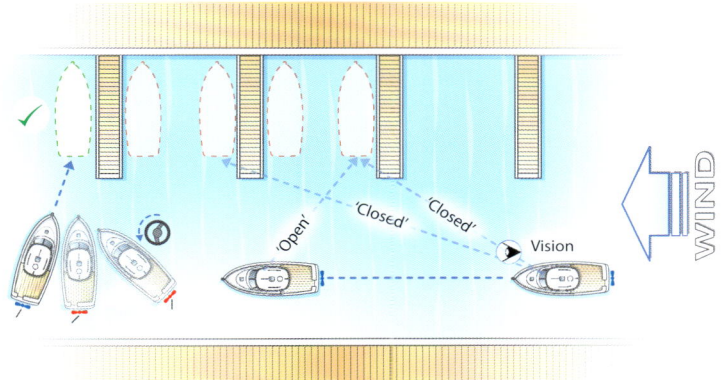

When the wind is blowing onto the berth, reversing in may be difficult as rapid movement of the bow is difficult to control ①. Starting from a downwind position, reverse into the wind and turn, which pushes the bow upwind, offsetting the wind pushing against it. Then reverse in ②.

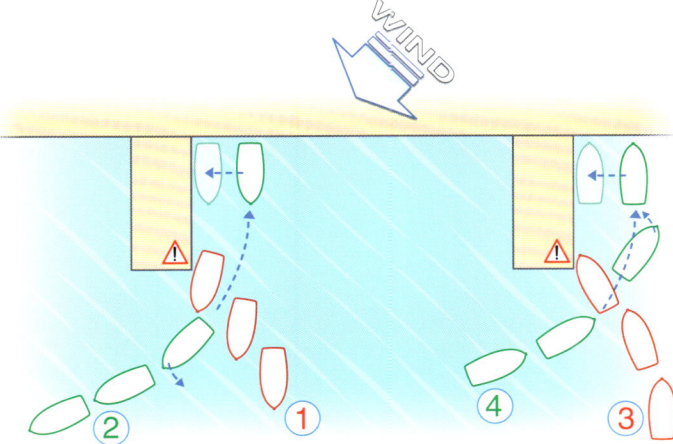

Another issue with the wind blowing onto the berth is that it may force the vessel sideways too quickly ③. As an alternative, motor up into the wind. Stop the vessel, then ease bow towards the berth and enter positively but before the wind creates sideways momentum. Arrest forward movement and drift alongside ④.

5 BOAT HANDLING

When the wind is blowing off the berth, reverse up into the wind then reverse into the berth to 'flick' the bow upwind. Careful timing is needed to allow the vessel to ease alongside, allowing lines to be deployed ⑤.

With the wind blowing off the berth, a risk is that the bow impacts an adjacent vessel if the approach allows the wind to grab control of the bow. Ideally, ease into position adjacent to the berth, balance the effect of the elements on the craft using the throttle and steering, and then drive into the berth ⑥.

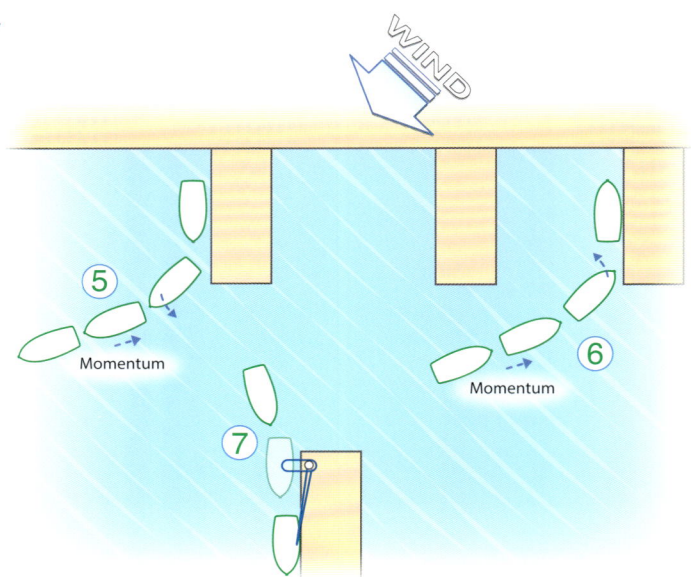

When entering a berth, first lasso the cleat, secure the line and then motor against the spring line to bring the craft alongside and hold the vessel in this position ⑦.

Lines should always be rigged before approaching a berth. In less favourable conditions, rig additional lines in case they are needed at short notice.

On many craft the midships cleat is underutilised. It may be easier to moor the craft initially using the stern line and midships line. Then, deal with the bow line when alongside as the stern and midships lines will hold the craft.

Always fender both sides of the craft well. Aim for the boat to be parallel to the berth so the fenders engage along the craft. Small adjustments of the throttle and steering are often necessary to 'tidy up' the vessel as it comes alongside.

In difficult conditions, choosing an easier berth and waiting for an improvement is the sign of a capable and confident skipper.

Tip: If it goes wrong, don't power out of a problem as any impact will be more severe. Reduce speed and don't fend off with limbs.

Tip: Slow is good. If all is going really well and you are drifting in alongside then just let it happen.

Finally, don't forget that it won't always be pretty. Just make sure it is always safe.

BOAT HANDLING | 5

Trim

At slow speed in windy conditions, trimming the bow down into the water using trim tabs or outdrives may help the vessel track through the water.

Care must be taken though, as if moving astern with the trim tabs down the tabs may be damaged and the boat may not steer predictably.

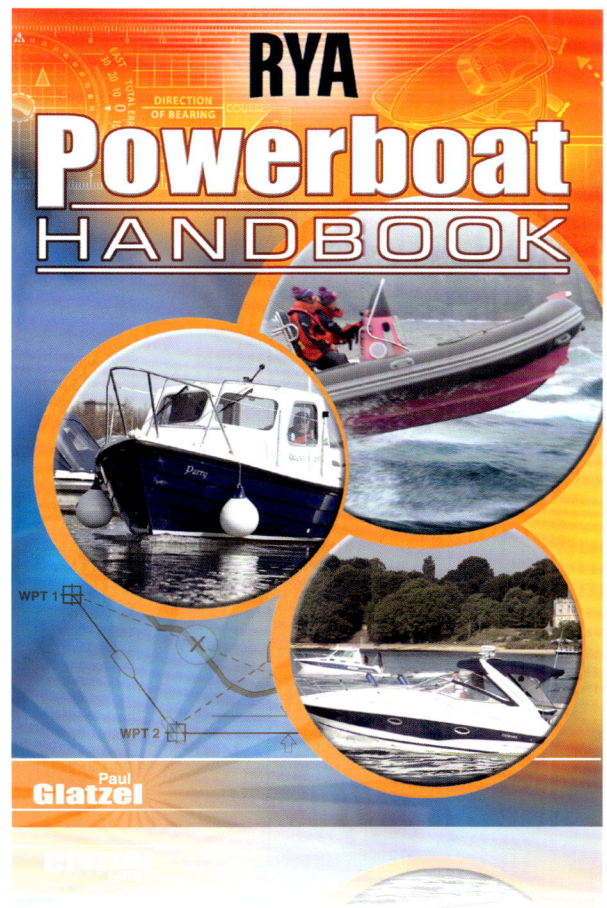

Chapters 6 (Boat Handling) and 7 (Leaving and Coming Alongside) from **G13 RYA Powerboat Handbook** are good further reading.

Chapter 6

Collision Regulations

The *International Regulations for Preventing Collisions at Sea* define how we must act to prevent collisions. Whether we refer to them as the 'ColRegs' or IRPCS we must fully understand and apply these rules.

Irrespective of our level of experience and qualification we have a legal responsibility to understand and apply the rules relevant to us.

As we progress as boaters then so our understanding and application of the rules must develop too. We will need to be comfortable with the actions of vessels in restricted visibility or understand the rules for vessels crossing or joining traffic separation schemes. Whatever our level of knowledge, reminding ourselves of the basics is always helpful. The key rules are:

- They apply to us all but common sense must prevail to prevent collisions. There is no 'right of way'.
- Rules are different for vessels 'in sight of each other' as opposed to when in or near restricted visibility.
- We must keep a good lookout 'by all available means' – sight, sound, radar, AIS – and at all times, even when single-handed. Most collisions occur because craft didn't see one another.
- Adopt a 'safe speed' considering visibility, sea state, proximity of other vessels, hazards, stopping, turning distances and any other relevant factor.
- Continually assess whether a 'risk of collision' exists.
- Understand that we, in power-driven craft, sit low in the hierarchy of vessels and will generally need to keep clear of other craft.
- Actions must be 'positive' and 'early'.

Too often collisions occur because skippers (even very experienced ones) fail to apply these very basic rules. There are no excuses.

Assessing the Risk of Collision

Determining whether the other vessel remains on a steady bearing (in which case a collision is inevitable) using a hand bearing compass is preferable, but is not always practical. Alternatively, line up two objects on your boat – perhaps a stanchion or other fitting – as a transit with the other boat.

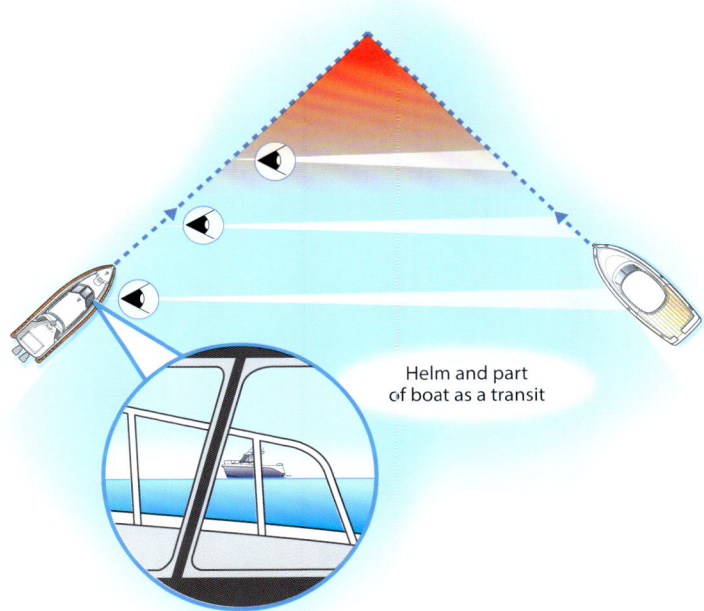

Helm and part of boat as a transit

Keeping Clear

Smaller power-driven craft are generally more manoeuvrable and less likely to be constrained in their movement. Turns should generally be to starboard, positive and early. Vessels should avoid passing ahead of other craft.

Power-driven vessels should keep clear of vessels:

- Not under command
- Restricted in their ability to manoeuvre
- Constrained by draught
- Engaged in fishing
- Sailing (including windsurfers, dinghies etc.)
- Kayaking, canoeing etc.

6 COLLISION REGULATIONS

Head-on: Power v. Power

Two power-driven vessels definitely or nearly head on – BOTH make 'early and positive' turns to starboard.

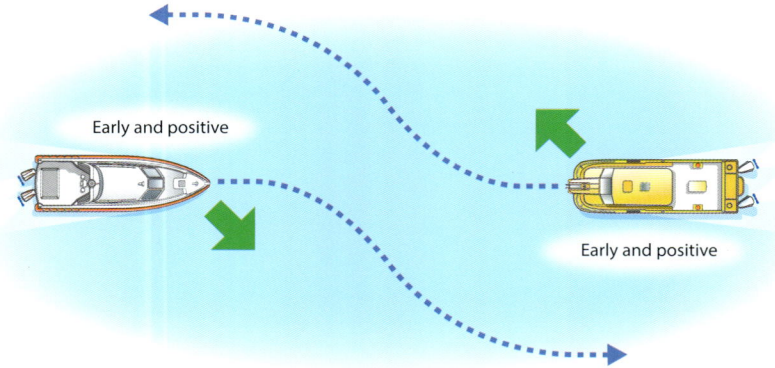

No rules require power-driven vessels to pass 'port to port'. If there is no risk of collision, avoid cutting across a vessel's bow as this creates a risk of collision!

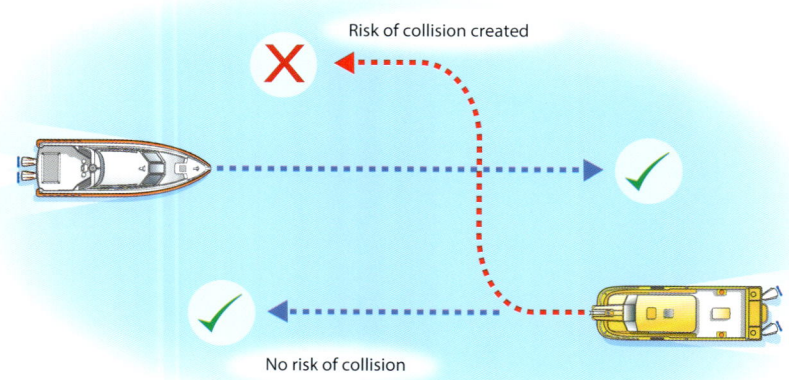

COLLISION REGULATIONS 6

Crossing Situation: Power v. Power

Where two power-driven vessels are crossing and a risk of collision exists, the vessel which has the other on her starboard side is the give-way vessel.

The 'stand-on' vessel must maintain course and speed and keep constant watch on the give-way vessel to take avoiding action if necessary.

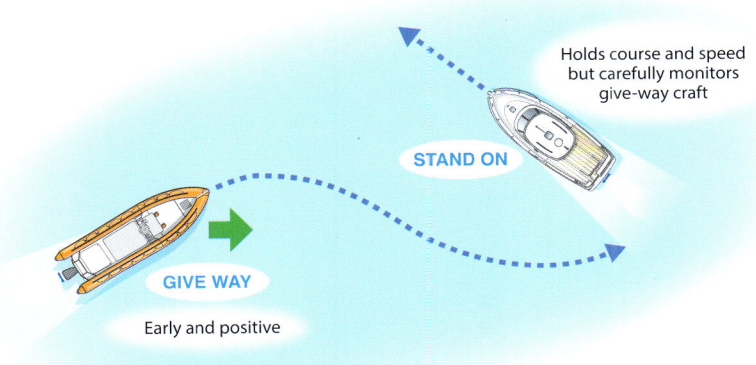

The 'stand-on' vessel must take action as soon as it is apparent the 'give-way' vessel is not acting as required. Slowing down is rarely enough and is not 'positive'. Turn away to starboard. Do not alter course to port. Consider stopping vessel.

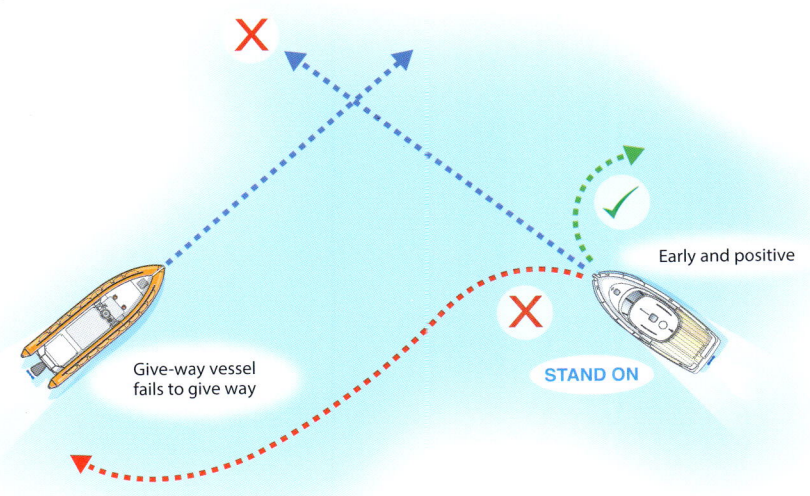

RYA ADVANCED POWERBOAT HANDBOOK

6 COLLISION REGULATIONS

Overtaking

A vessel in an arc of 135° at the stern of another is 'overtaking' and is the 'give-way' vessel. The vessel being overtaken is the 'stand-on' vessel. The overtaking vessel must not cut in until 'past and clear'. Sailing boats overtaking power-driven craft are 'give-way'.

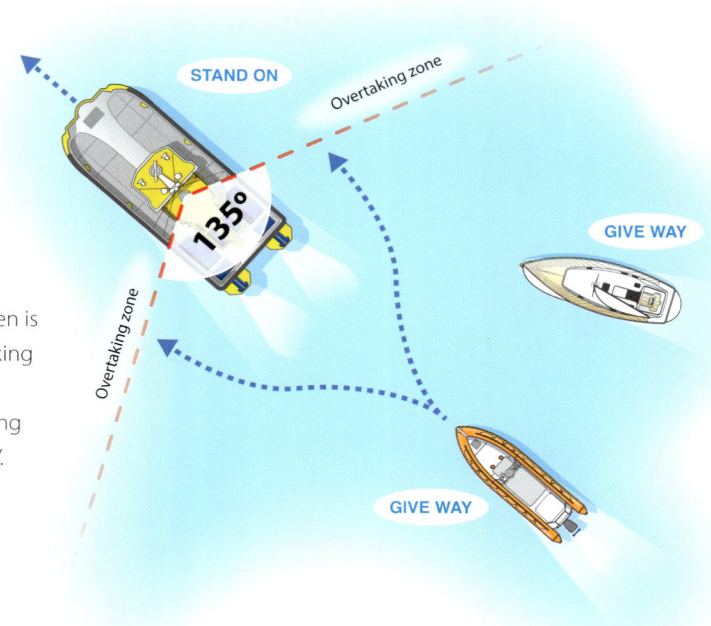

Sail v. Sail

A sail boat using its engine becomes a 'power-driven vessel' and should display a motor sailing cone.

If under sail alone:
vessels on different tacks –
the starboard-tack vessel
is stand on and
port-tack vessel
gives way.

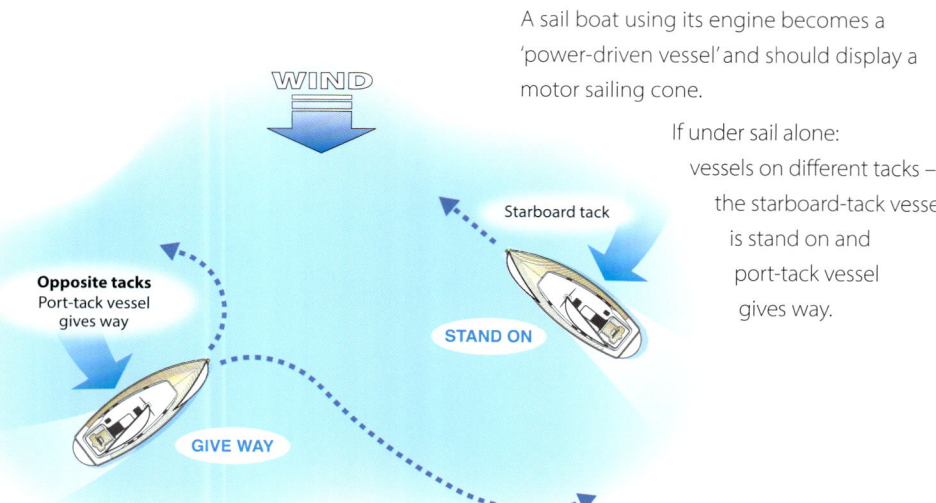

COLLISION REGULATIONS | 6

Vessels on the same tack – the vessel nearest the wind (to 'windward') is the give-way vessel.

A vessel is on port tack when the wind is blowing into its sails over the port side of the vessel. When the wind is coming over the starboard side, it is on starboard tack.

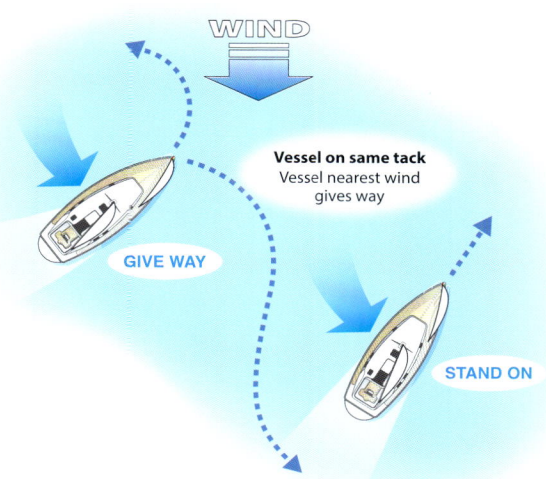

Narrow Channels and Traffic Separation Schemes (TSS)

Keep clear of narrow channels if possible. If a vessel is limited by its draught to a channel, do not impede it. If overtaking, be sure there is room and emit sound signals. At a bend in the channel, be careful and emit sound signals.

If possible, stay clear of Traffic Separation Schemes and use inshore channels. If joining a TSS, do so at a 'small angle'. Never impede a vessel and if you must cross, do so at right angles to the TSS.

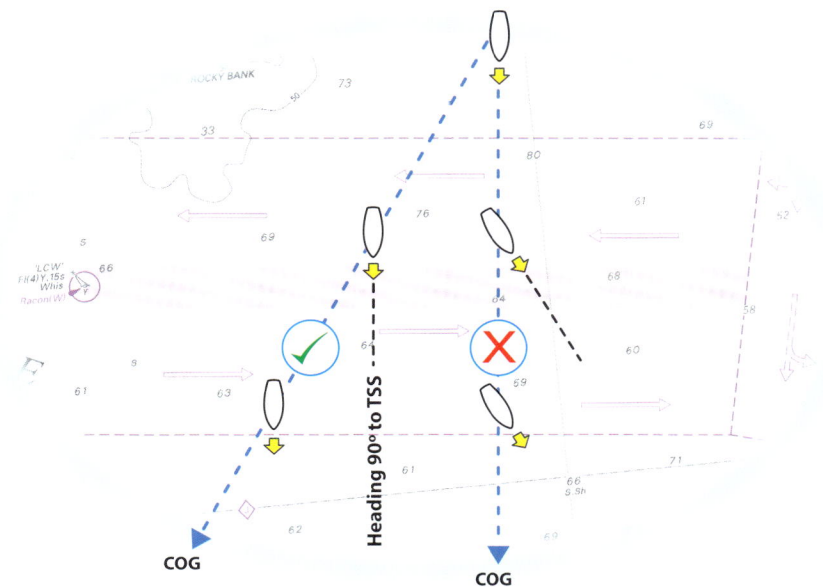

6 COLLISION REGULATIONS

Restricted Visibility

The actions already described are for vessels 'in sight of one another' – visually, day or night but not by radar alone. When in (or near) an area of restricted visibility the rules change.

Common sense dictates, and the rules state, that vessels must progress at a safe speed, sound the appropriate signals and switch navigation lights on. In practice, this means slowing to the vessel's minimum practical speed (and if necessary stopping) and also keeping a very good lookout.

Vessels without Radar

The rules state that if you hear a fog signal that seems ahead of you, then you should slow to minimum speed and 'navigate with extreme caution' until the danger has passed.

In practice this means you should be ready to take immediate avoiding action if it becomes clear where the other vessel is relative to you.

Vessels with Radar

The rules place an obligation on vessels fitted with radar to use it and to do so properly.

For vessels 'seen' on radar alone the actions you should take are best summarised visually.

Tip: A radar course is almost essential if you want to understand how to use it properly.

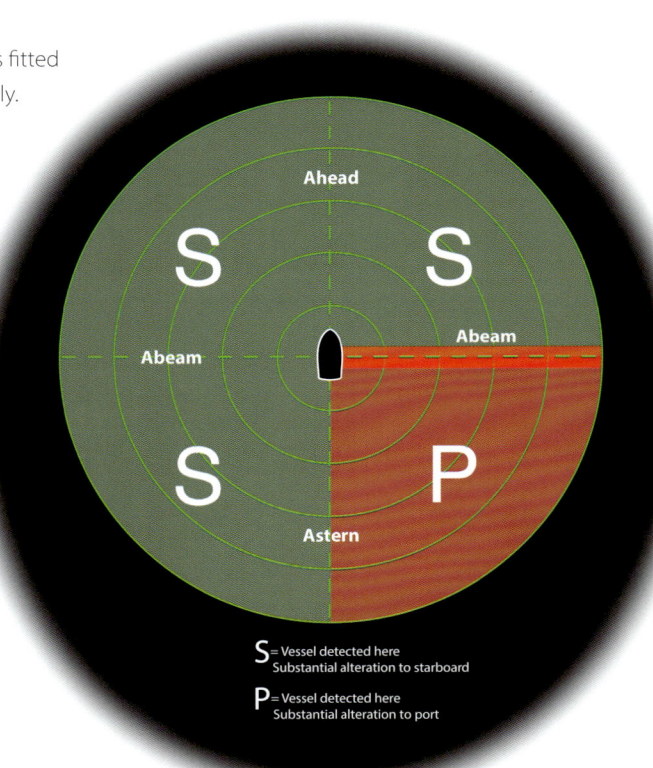

S = Vessel detected here
Substantial alteration to starboard

P = Vessel detected here
Substantial alteration to port

When operating in restricted visibility, small craft should keep clear of shipping channels and consider anchoring in shallow water. Wear lifejackets and keep a good lookout – switching off the engine may help you to hear other craft.

42 RYA ADVANCED POWERBOAT HANDBOOK

COLLISION REGULATIONS 6

Lights, Day Shapes and Sound Signals

At night a skipper needs to be able to identify quickly the types of vessel they can see so they can make the correct decisions according to the collision regulations. During daylight, day shapes indicate that a vessel's movement is constrained in some way – recognising these and reacting appropriately is of critical importance.

To determine what the lights that they can see represent, a skipper should develop a method so they can recognise vessels quickly. Adopting an approach where they pose themselves a series of questions can work well:

Q: Is the vessel under power or sail?
A: The lights shown allow clear distinction between sail and power.

Lights displayed	Power-driven vessels	Sailing vessels
Port and starboard sidelights	Yes – optional for vessels under 7m and 7 knots. Vessels under 20m can combine sidelights into a 'bi-colour' light at the bow	Yes – vessels under 20m can combine sidelights into a 'bi-colour' light at the bow
Stern light	Yes – if over 12m. Under 12m may be combined with a masthead light	Yes – sailing vessels under 20m can combine port, starboard and stern lights into a tri-colour at the top of the mast
Masthead light	Yes – masthead and stern light may be combined for vessels less than 12m	No

Remember, though, that a sailing vessel becomes a power-driven vessel when propelling itself with its engine. It will be fitted with the light combinations for both sail and power but should only display those accurately representing what it is doing.

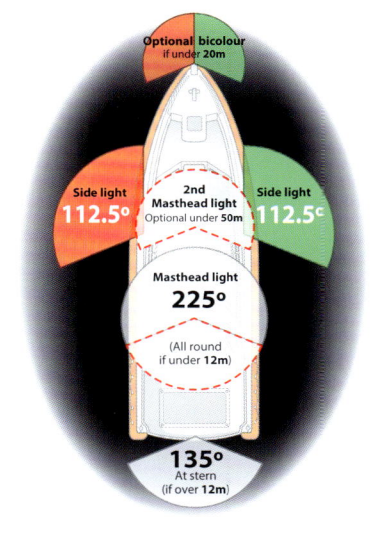

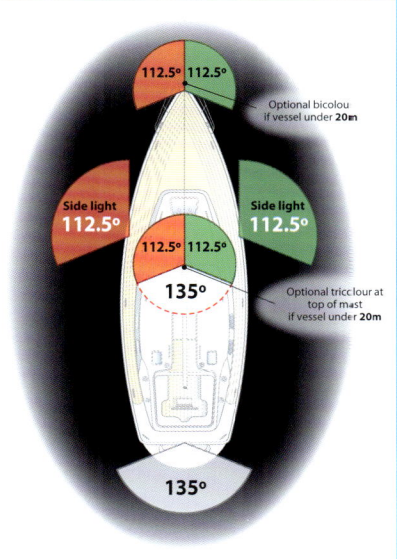

6 COLLISION REGULATIONS

Q: How large is the vessel?
A: For power-driven vessels a craft is either definitely under 50m or probably over 50m.

Lights displayed	Power-driven vessels	Sailing vessels
Additional masthead light	Yes and no. Optional under 50m, mandatory over 50m	No. Cannot determine length of vessel from lights

Q: What is the direction of travel?
A: Determine from which lights are visible.

Q: Is the vessel doing anything?
A: On power-driven vessels, additional lights are added to indicate the vessel is undertaking a task or is restricted in its movement in some way. The corresponding day shapes are shown alongside the lights where relevant.

More common ones are:

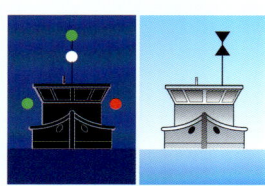

Vessel fishing with nets (trawling) – all-round white and green when under way plus sidelights and stern light when making way

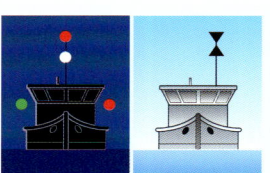

Vessel fishing but not trawling – all-round white and red when under way plus sidelights and stern light when making way

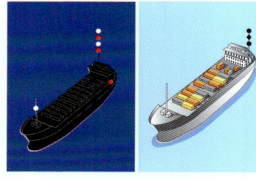

Restricted in ability to manoeuvre ('RAM') – all-round red-white-red lights when under way plus sidelights, masthead and stern light when making way

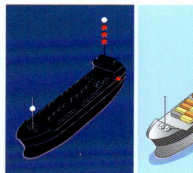

Constrained by draught ('CBD') – three all-round red lights in addition to sidelights, masthead and stern light denoting vessel under way

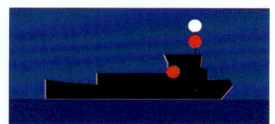

Pilot vessel – all-round white and red lights plus sidelights and stern light denoting vessel under way

Air-cushioned vessel operating in non-displacement mode. Lights are also often used for very-high-speed ferries

Towing under 200m – an additional masthead light plus an additional yellow towing light above the sternlight. If the vessel is severely restricted in ability to manoeuvre then it additionally displays 'Restricted in Ability to Manoeuvre' lights

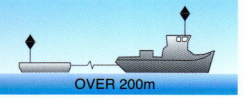

Towing over 200m – two additional masthead lights plus an additional yellow towing light above the sternlight. If the vessel is severely restricted in ability to manoeuvre then it additionally displays 'Restricted in Ability to Manoeuvre' lights

COLLISION REGULATIONS 6

Other light combinations and day shapes include:

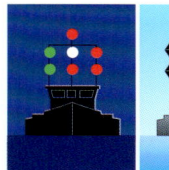 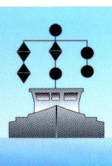 Vessel engaged in underwater operations or with gear out – two all-round red lights indicating the area of the obstruction whilst two all-round green lights indicate the safe side to pass. Sidelights, masthead and stern light when making way

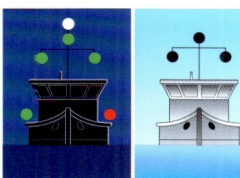 Vessel engaged in mine clearance operations shall additionally display three all-round green lights plus sidelights, masthead and stern light indicating under way

  Not under command ('NUC') – two all-round red lights when under way, plus sidelights and stern light when making way

Vessel with divers down. 'Flag' should actually be a rigid structure of 1m²

Q: Is the vessel under way or making way?

> **Definitions:**
> Under way: Not attached to shore or the ground in any way
> Making way: Being propelled through the water by sail or power

A: Generally, the lights that a vessel displays only show that a craft is under way. The combination of some lights indicating an activity or constraint with sidelights, a masthead light and a stern light indicates the vessel is making way. This applies to:

- *Vessel fishing with nets (trawling)*
- *Vessel fishing but not trawling*
- *Vessel restricted in ability to manoeuvre*
- *Vessel not under command*

RYA ADVANCED POWERBOAT HANDBOOK

6 COLLISION REGULATIONS

So in practice this means that for a vessel undertaking the 'activity' above, showing just the lights relevant to the activity in the list (without sidelights, a masthead light and a stern light) means that it is under way, whilst adding the sidelights, a masthead light and a stern light means it is making way.

When at anchor:

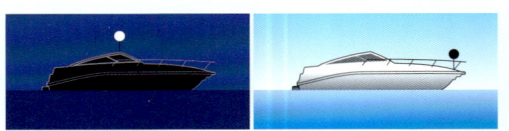

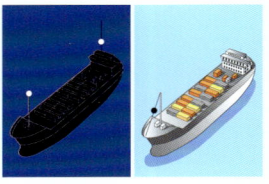

At anchor over 50m – all-round white lights at bow and stern, higher at bow than stern

At anchor under 50m – all-round white light

Positioning and visibility of lights is very specific. Lights must be a certain brightness according to vessel size, with positioning of lights specified too.

COLLISION REGULATIONS | 6

Sound Signals

- Short blast = one second
- Long blast = four–six seconds

MANOEUVRING AND WARNING SIGNALS

One short blast
I am turning
to starboard.

Two short blasts
I am turning
to port.

Three short blasts
My engines are
going astern.

**Five or more
short blasts**
Your intentions are
not understood.

OVERTAKING

**Two long and one
short blasts**
I wish to pass you
to starboard.
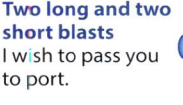

**Two long and two
short blasts**
I wish to pass you
to port.

Morse Code 'C'
I agree to you
passing.

IN RESTRICTED VISIBILITY

One long blast
Sound every two
minutes to
indicate a power
vessel making way.

Two long blasts
Sound every two
minutes to signify
a power vessel
stopped.
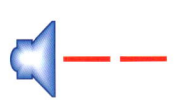

**One long and 2
short blasts**
Sound every two
minutes to indicate a
sail vessel making way.
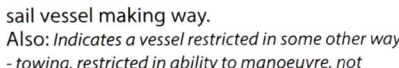
Also: *Indicates a vessel restricted in some other way
- towing, restricted in ability to manoeuvre, not
under command, constrained by draught.*

AT ANCHOR
Not more than every minute

Vessel at anchor
Rapid ringing of bell for
5 seconds every minute.

Vessel at anchor over 100m
Bell rung forward. Then gong
rung rapidly for 5 seconds aft.

Vessel aground
Three rings of bell + Anchor
signals + Three rings of bell.

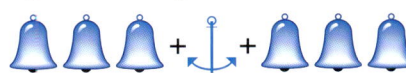

One short, one long, one short blast
Any vessel, optional.

Tip: More detailed information about all aspects of the IRPCS can be found in the book G2 RYA International Regulations for Preventing Collisions at Sea (Melanie Bartlett).

Chapter 7

Navigation

Navigating in smaller craft at any speed should embrace the full range of navigation techniques, from integrating electronics to the use of a compass, depth, speed and time. Preparation is key and the skipper must choose the most relevant methods according to the passage being undertaken, the likely speed, the available kit and the craft they are on.

To create an effective and safe plan you must have a good understanding of charts, tides, buoyage and the variety of navigational techniques available to you. This chapter assumes that you already have developed an understanding of these areas and seek to build on this knowledge.

This chapter should be read in conjunction with the chapters on navigation within the RYA Powerboat Handbook (G13) and RYA Start Powerboating (G48).

NAVIGATION 7

Planning a Passage

Safety of Life at Sea Chapter 5 (SOLAS V) makes it a legal requirement to plan a passage when going to sea. The format of our plan and the issues considered relevant are up to us and we must ensure that our plan is realistic and any risks associated with it are managed and acceptable.

When navigating between two locations we must consider a variety of factors to ensure the safety of our crew and craft:

- **People:** Are you, the crew and the passengers capable? Is the equipment/clothing and everyone's experience/knowledge/training suitable?
- **Weather:** Is there a 'weather window'? Consider localised conditions – 'wind against tide'. Will entry to ports be possible? On longer passages on slower craft, weather changes can occur during the passage – has this been considered?
- **Craft:** Is the vessel suitable, seaworthy, and capable of dealing with predicted conditions? Is it well maintained, reliable (and has it been used recently?), and carrying spares and tools? Are appropriate lifesaving appliances for the passage and area carried?
- **Communication:** Have you told the Coastguard, marina or friends/family? Are boat/vessel details registered with rescue services?

The plan itself divides into two elements:

- **Pilotage:** The exit from (and subsequent entry to) a marina, harbour or estuary where the craft is close to shore and there are many navigational references available (e.g. buoyage, buildings, shoreline, depth etc.).
- **Open-water passage:** The part of the passage between the pilotage needed at either end of the passage.

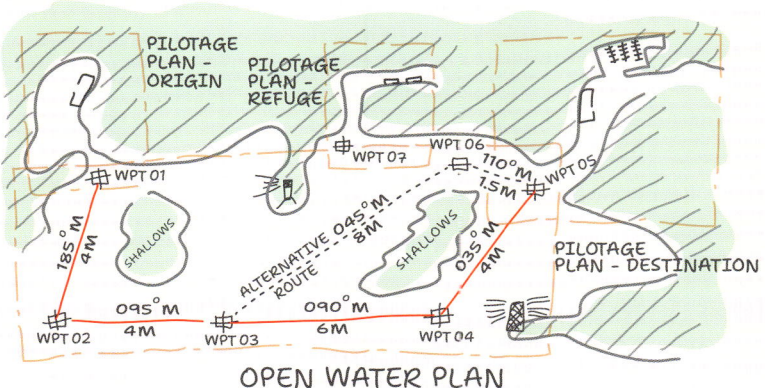

7 NAVIGATION

Many passages that are made in smaller craft utilise pilotage techniques from departure to arrival.
Navigational techniques will be used to:

- Follow the route from the departure point to the destination.
- Confirm position along the route – 'position fixing'.

Some techniques help us follow this route and provide a position, while others are more suited to pilotage than the open-water element and vice-versa.

An integrated approach should be adopted, marrying the most relevant electronic techniques to non-electronic methods. No part of a plan should ever rely on just one technique; a good plan will usually have a primary method of travelling the route with two or three other methods to back it up.

Key aspects of safe and effective navigation are preparation and, if there are two or more persons aboard, the communication between the navigator and helm.

If alone, the helm's plan must be clear, simple and easy to read in a small, fast-moving craft. Turn points and dangers should be clear and progress smooth, with the helm able to think ahead. With a person operating as navigator the commands must be clear and acknowledged. The helm must know what they need to do before arrival, e.g. "In one minute turn to 200° magnetic, line up with two yellow posts in transit...".

The Pilotage Plan

Pilotage is the navigation of a vessel within close proximity to land, such as in harbours and estuaries, where there are likely to be various aids to navigation such as bucyage, distinct structures ashore, varying depths and a distinctive shoreline. All passages will start and finish with some pilotage, although in some locations this could be really simple. Some passages never really leave an area where pilotage techniques are used, so use pilotage for the entire passage.

As skipper, at the planning stage you must choose which techniques work best to enter the port, harbour or marina depending on what is available and what the risks are. A combination of techniques is best.

Why not just use a chartplotter and follow the channels?

While there is no doubt that a chartplotter is beneficial, it is important to understand its limitations. A Global Navigation Satellite System (GNSS)/chartplotter unit can be assumed to be accurate to 15m 95 per cent of the time. A problem afloat is knowing when an error occurs and the difference is greater than 15m. In a vehicle an error in a satellite navigation system is obvious but afloat we may not spot it, and adjusting position may lead us to adjust our position incorrectly. In open water offshore this may not be a problem, but when navigating a narrow channel into a harbour such an adjustment could lead you into real danger.

The paper charts we use are produced by a government's hydrographic office (or another organisation licensed by them) and can be assumed to be accurate. The electronic charts produced for chartplotters, laptops and tablets/smartphones may not be as accurate, which is why when switching on electronic charts you must agree that "this product's features cannot be relied upon as complete or accurate".

NAVIGATION 7

Therefore, solely using a chartplotter to navigate a narrow channel into an unfamiliar port without creating a pilotage plan to use alongside it should be avoided.

Usually a visual representation is preferable. Drawing the plan:

- Lifts the key details from the chart
- Helps to identify the key landmarks and dangers on entry
- Helps to commit the plan to memory

Always have a chart available for additional information and remember to produce pilotage plans for ports of refuge along a route.

Open-water and pilotage plans can be drawn up and laminated, with space to record variants
– such as weather and tidal-related information – and then used again for the same area.

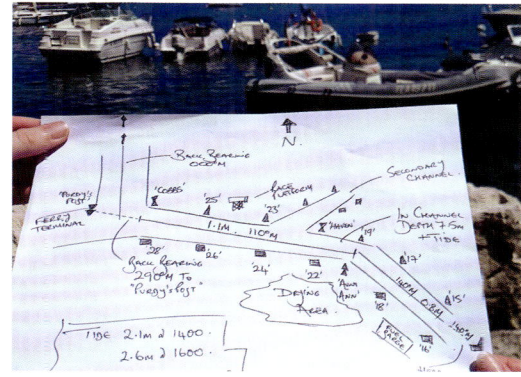

Pilotage Techniques

You must ensure the charted objects you have chosen are lit or visible if you are planning to use them at night.

Transits

Line up two objects to keep you on your intended track.

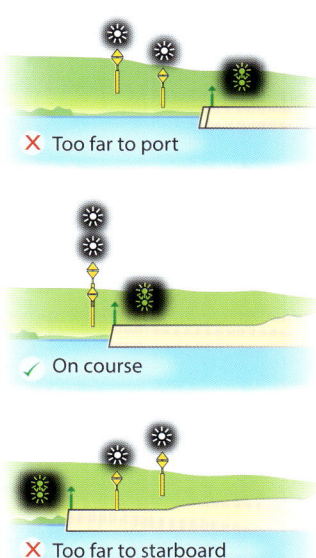

RYA ADVANCED POWERBOAT HANDBOOK   51

7 NAVIGATION

Bearing and Distance

Measure a bearing, convert to a magnetic heading and steer, following your compass. Over longer distances it is easy to head a few degrees off your intended track.

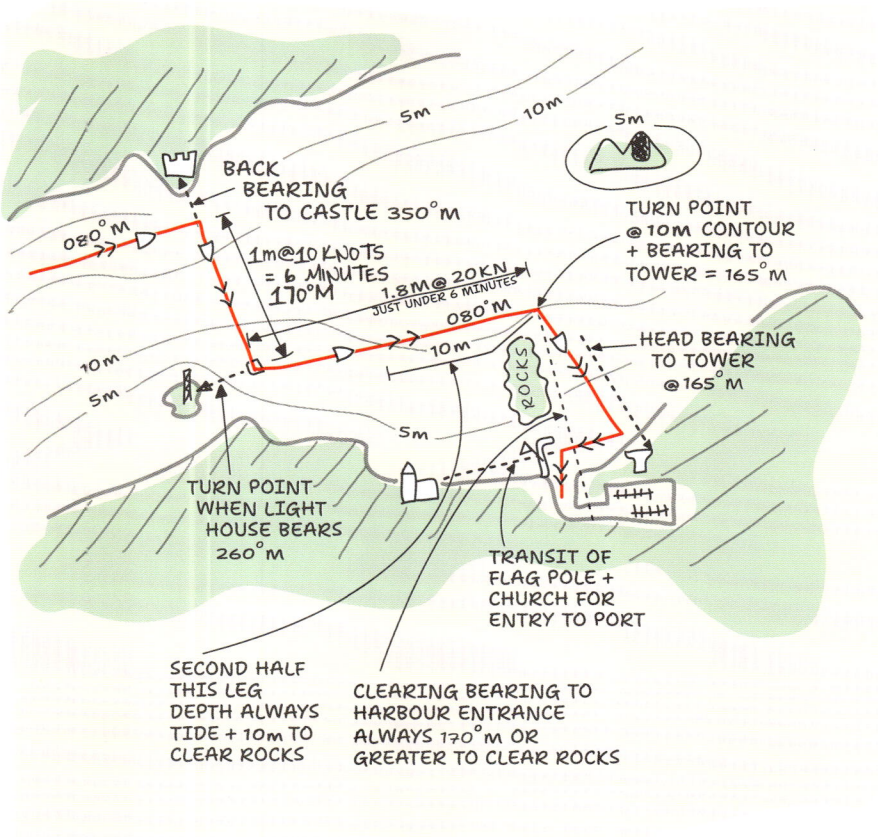

Clearing Lines and Bearings

Define safe or dangerous areas. A waypoint and a GNSS/chartplotter can be used in preference to a compass to create an electronic clearing bearing.

Back Bearing

Calculate the bearing back to an object. This is a simple way to stay on your intended track and counters the effects of tide and wind pushing the vessel off course.

Head Bearing

This is similar to a back bearing but is forward of the vessel.

RYA ADVANCED POWERBOAT HANDBOOK

NAVIGATION 7

Cross Bearings
This is a bearing to an object to port or starboard of the vessel. It can be used to identify a turn point.

Turn Points
A point identified for a change of heading. You can use a combination of the previous techniques.

Depth and Contour Lines
Contour lines can be used to navigate along or may be used to indicate turn points or general position.

Speed/Time/Distance
By calculating the time taken at a certain speed to cover a known distance you can time your arrival at a point. This could be a turn point or, again, a general position.

Radar (see also Chapter 8)
Parallel indexing: A line is positioned parallel to the intended track to ensure your vessel clears the shore or a headland by the required distance. Note that caution should be exercised as low shorelines and tidal height may result in the reflected target being further inland than the charted shoreline.

Clearing ranges: Set the Variable Range Marker (VRM) to a predetermined range. Keep the VRM touching the shore to remain at that distance. In the example this is set to 0.3M. This can be difficult to manage at speed. Consider setting two VRMs, for example at 0.3M and 0.7M, and endeavour to keep the land within that safety range.

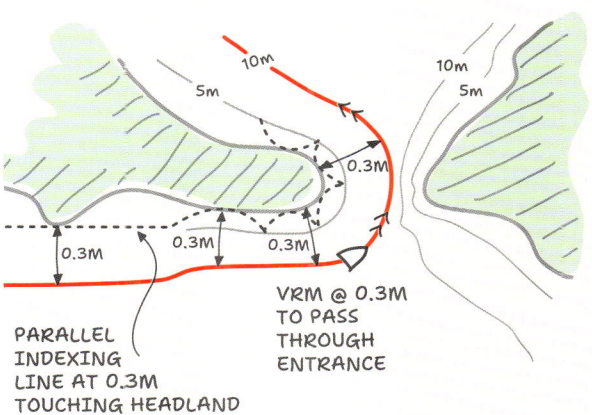

7 NAVIGATION

Understanding the Light Characteristics of Buoyage

Navigating at night requires that you can quickly identify buoyage and lit features from their light characteristics.

There are various ways in which a feature/buoy may be lit:

NAME	CHART SYMBOL	DESCRIPTION	VISUALLY
Fixed	F	Fixed light – always on	
Flashing	Fl	Flashing, off more than on	
Group flashing	Fl (2)	Flashing in groups	
Long flashing	LFl	Flashing, off more than on but lasting 2 or more seconds	
Quick	Q	50-79 flashes per min	
Very quick	VQ	80-90 flashes per min	
Group quick	Q (9)	A group of quick flashes followed by a period off	
Interrupted quick	IQ	Similar to group quick but with no specified number of flashes	
Isophase	Iso	Equally on and off	
Occulting	Oc	More on than off	
Alternating	Al.WR	Colour changes	
Fixed and flashing	F Fl(2)	Fixed light with flahses at higher intensity	

The colour, the number of flashes and the time period of each sequence will also vary.

This variety allows the identification of specific lights when afloat at night. Identifying the characteristics of a light when afloat and then finding that same light on the chart can be difficult, however. Preparing a plan ahead of going afloat makes this far easier.

If boating close to built-up areas, lights that are ashore are easily confused with those afloat.

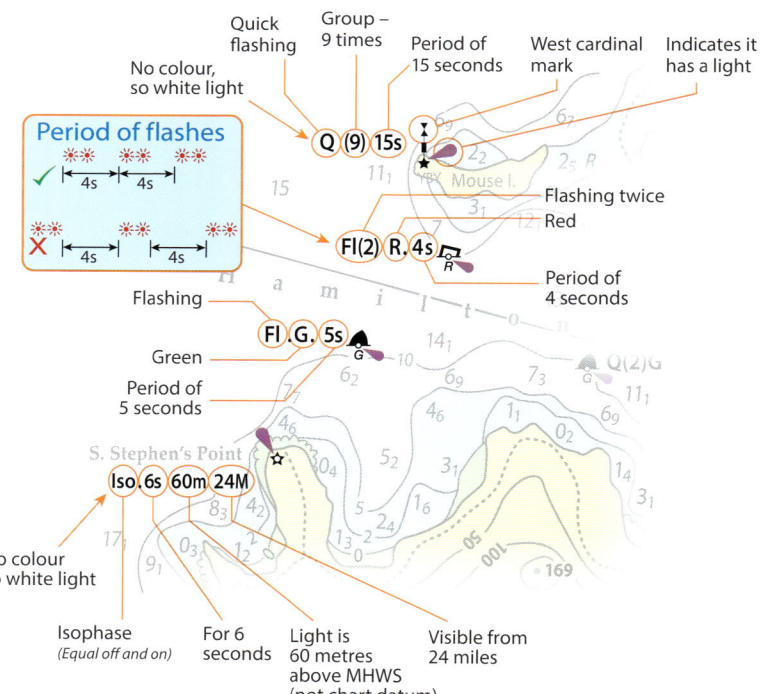

54 RYA ADVANCED POWERBOAT HANDBOOK

NAVIGATION 7

The Open-water Plan

An effective open-water plan:

- Overlaps with the pilotage plans at either end of the route.
- Shows waypoints and routes in addition to the required course and distances to travel.
- Highlights ports of refuge.
- Details tidal and weather information.
- Highlights tidal windows/gates and key dangers along a route.

Many of the previously detailed techniques that are used for pilotage work well for the open-water element of the passage.

Waypoints and Routes

A waypoint may be a position to navigate to, an area of danger to keep clear of, or one of a number of waypoints to link together to form a route between two points.

Enter waypoints into a chartplotter/GNSS unit using latitude/longitude or by positioning a cursor at the required position. Never assume waypoints found in almanacs and nautical guides are correct – always check. Reposition waypoints when taken from a pre-printed list to avoid multiple vessels arriving at the same point. Don't place on buoyage.

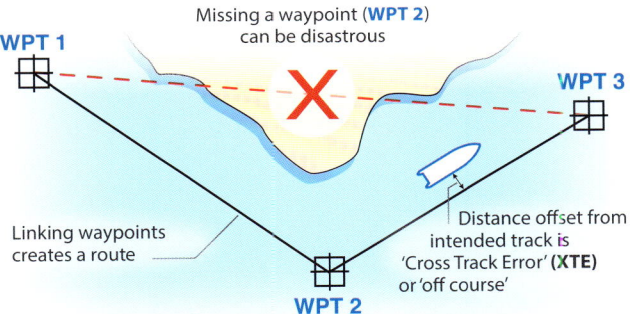

Make intelligent waypoints which are verifiable by sight (like turnpoints). Bear in mind that in reality you will arrive at a waypoint before the chartplotter updates and shows you have. Similarly, relying on your GNSS's compass display when at a turnpoint can lead to over-turning while the system updates. Use the steering compass in this instance.

Routes are created either by adding waypoints to a route or by moving a cursor between two locations, clicking to enter the waypoints as you go.

Decide on an acceptable 'Cross Track Error' (XTE or 'off course'). Ensure no dangers lurk too close on either side. Reposition the route if necessary. On the chartplotter screen, scroll in and run the cursor along the route to ensure no dangers are close to the intended track.

Waypoints can usually be moved by hovering the cursor over the waypoint, selecting 'Move' and then dragging it into a new position.

Additional waypoints can be inserted into a route either by adding them from a list or by landing on the route and selecting 'Insert waypoint'.

All chartplotters vary slightly. It is worth spending time with yours to understand how to create and amend waypoints and routes.

7 NAVIGATION

Proximity Waypoints

A 'normal' waypoint is typically a point that you want to travel to. A proximity waypoint is a point that you want to avoid. They can be used in two ways:

Perhaps there is an unlit buoy or a small rock in the area you boat or along your intended passage. Enter a waypoint in the usual way but change the symbol for that waypoint to something distinctive – for example, a skull and crossbones. Name it 'Rock'. It will then appear in a distinctive way on your plotter screen.

Alternatively, if there is a rock or headland you wish to keep a certain distance off, you could enter a waypoint there. 'Goto' the waypoint and show 'Distance to waypoint' on the screen. Simply keep that distance greater than the minimum you are happy with.

This method works best when you have a second plotter or a small handheld unit, leaving the main unit for 'normal' use.

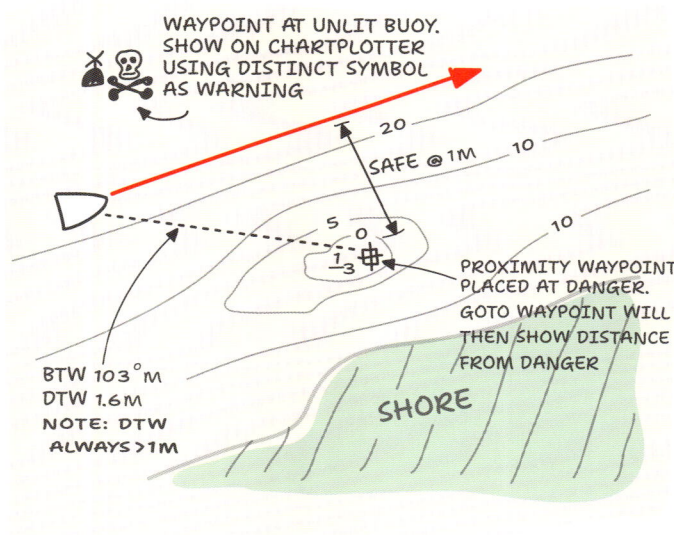

Fixing your Position

It is common sense to plot your position regularly on a chart in case the systems on board fail or visibility reduces. An estimate of current position can be made from a previous position fix and heading/speed/time/tide data.

Some of the pilotage methods introduced can be used to plot your position. Others include:

Visually: Keep it simple. If you are sure you are next to a known position then that's where you are! Make sure you are right though.

NAVIGATION 7

Bearings: Bearings can be used in combination with a transit, a radar range, a depth contour or on their own using the 'three-point fix' technique.

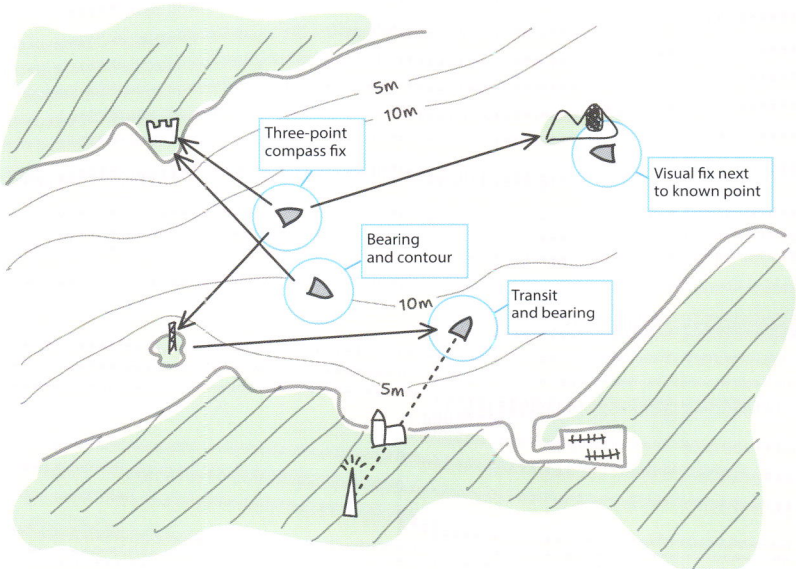

Radar: Radar offers excellent ways to position fix.

- Radar ranges – Use the Variable Range Marker (VRM) to measure distance very accurately. Plot ranges or to chart.
- Radar bearings – Use the Electronic Bearing Line (EBL) to measure bearings to objects.
- Radar image – Keep it simple. Matching the radar image of a bay or feature to the chartplotter may indicate position.

See also Chapter 8.

GNSS/chartplotters: Record atitude and longitude, heading, speed and time.

Waypoint web: A web drawn from a waypoint, showing bearing lines and arcs of distance, can be used to transit an area or to enter a port/harbour using the web to 'funnel' in. It is very simple to plot the position afloat.

7 NAVIGATION

Waypoint ladder: Parallel lines (representing cross-track error) either side of the route between two waypoints, and a scale along the route showing distance remaining to the destination, allow rapid and simple position-fixing using distance to destination and cross-track error. This is an excellent technique for the open-water element of the passage. Mark up the chart with the ladder and then plot the position regularly.

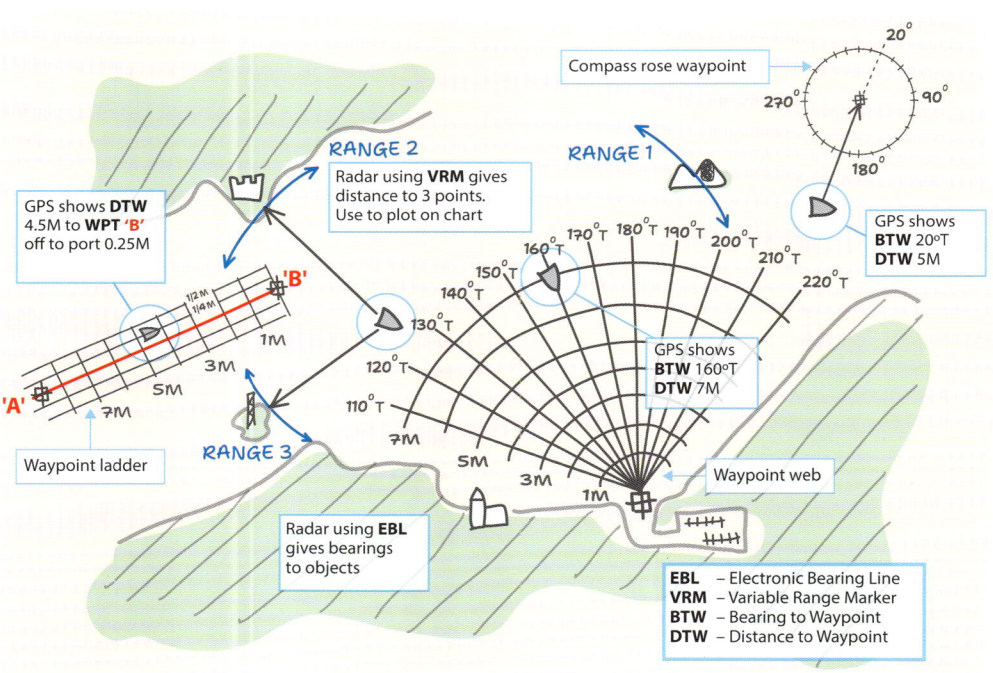

Compass rose waypoint: A simple and very effective means of position fixing. Enter a waypoint at the centre of a compass rose. 'Goto' that waypoint using a GNSS. Use the bearing and distance to the waypoint to plot your position.

NAVIGATION 7

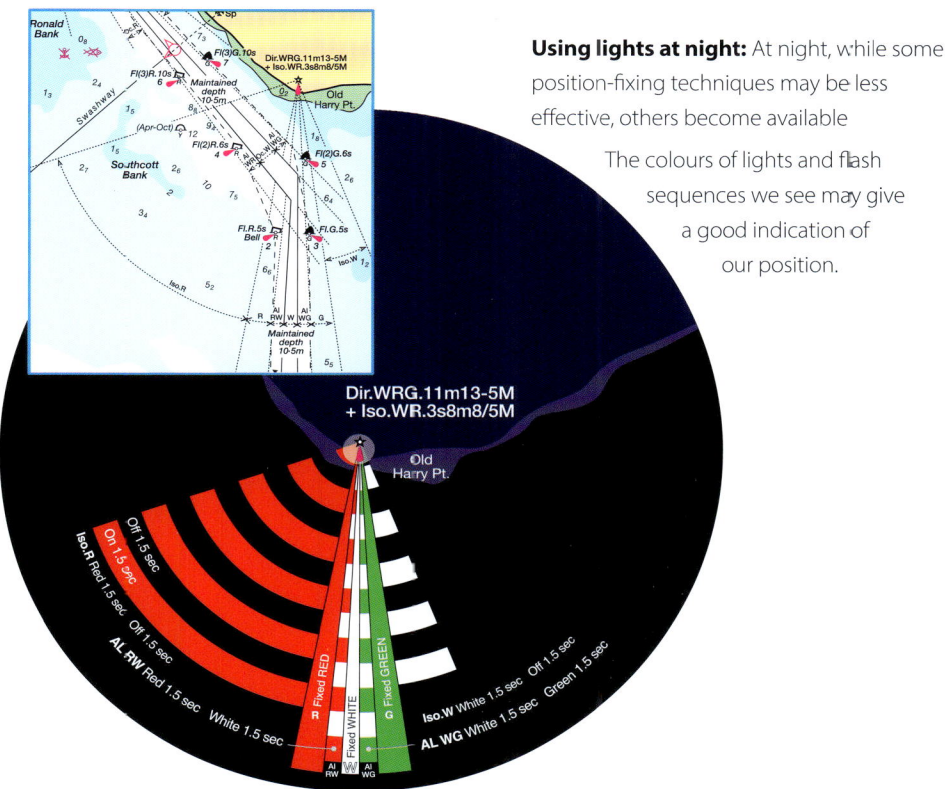

Using lights at night: At night, while some position-fixing techniques may be less effective, others become available

The colours of lights and flash sequences we see may give a good indication of our position.

Estimating Position

The position we plot on a chart as we travel our route should include course, speed and the time the plot occurred. If systems fail and you need to recalculate your new position manually, this will be from that last-known position.

Dead reckoning: Plot the position, draw on the vessel's heading at that time and use its speed and the time since the last plot to mark off distance travelled.

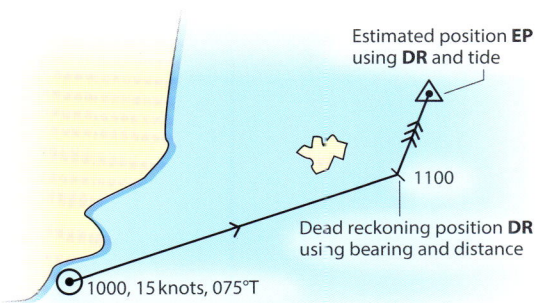

RYA ADVANCED POWERBOAT HANDBOOK

7 NAVIGATION

Estimated position: For the time travelled, calculate the rate and direction of the tidal stream and add this on to the position plotted, calculated using dead reckoning. This gives a more accurate position known as an 'Estimated Position'. If wind is significant then a 5°–10° adjustment – 'leeway' – should be applied to the water track.

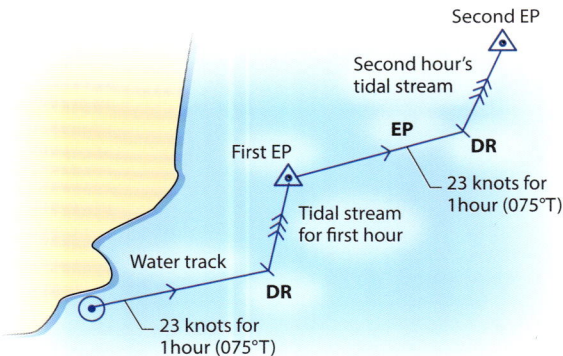

Multiple 'EPs' can be combined over longer time periods. Care should be taken as error may creep into each EP, reducing accuracy.

Calculating the Effect of Stream and Wind on Your Passage

Using a GNSS to navigate from A and B if the stream is trying to push the boat off course will ensure that you follow a straight path to B, but this will not always be the most efficient way of getting there.

For example, take a 30-mile passage at 10 knots taking roughly three hours. During the first hour the tide is from the east, during the second hour it is almost slack, and then it is coming from the west in hour three.

Following the straight A–B line using waypoints or a route means in hours one and three the vessel is fighting the tide (and expending fuel) to stay on the A–B line. Using the technique 'course to steer' you can calculate the heading that you should adopt throughout the passage that ensures you reach B, but not by travelling along the A–B line. You travel further but use less fuel.

Be careful to ensure no dangers exist near the track the vessel follows.

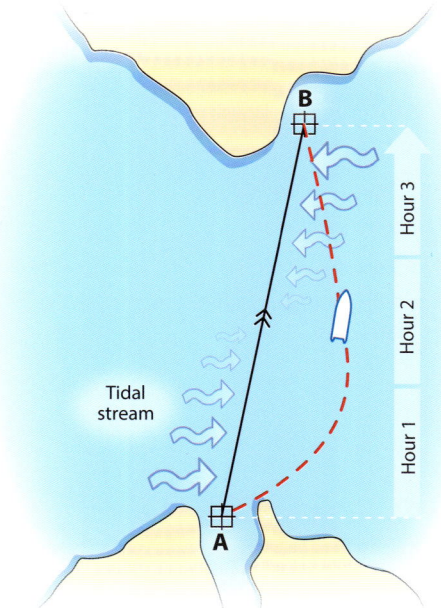

Calculating a 'Course to Steer'

- Draw line from A to B and beyond.

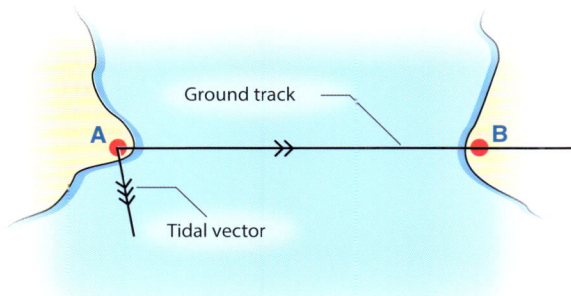

- This is your intended ground track (the two arrows are like two feet).
- At 'A', draw in the tidal vector.
- From the end of the tidal vector, mark off along the A–B line how far the vessel would travel in one hour (e.g. at 12 knots it would travel 12 nautical miles). The point at which this intersects the A–B line is C.
- Join the end of the tidal vector to C. This is the water track. Use a plotter to measure the bearing – this is the Course to Steer (CTS).
- Remember not to join the end of the tidal vector directly to B – this would be wrong.

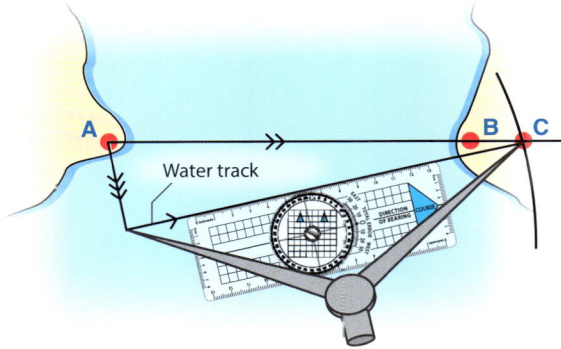

- Distance A–C is the actual distance travelled in one hour – this equates to Speed Over Ground (SOG). In this example the tidal vector is pointing slightly towards B, increasing the vessel's SOG.
- This example assumes a passage of roughly one hour's duration, so the amount of tidal vector chosen was one hour. Plotting over a 30-minute period achieves the same results, as does using any other timescale or unit of measurement. For example, instead of measuring 2.3 knots for the tidal vector, you could measure 2.3cm, and 12.6cm instead of a boat speed of 12.6 knots when plotting the A–C line. Using alternative units may make the course to steer easier to draw.

7 NAVIGATION

Course to Steer over more than One Hour

On longer passages multiple tidal vectors may need to be plotted. Be careful though, as predicting the actual ground track may indicate the vessel passes too close to a potential danger.

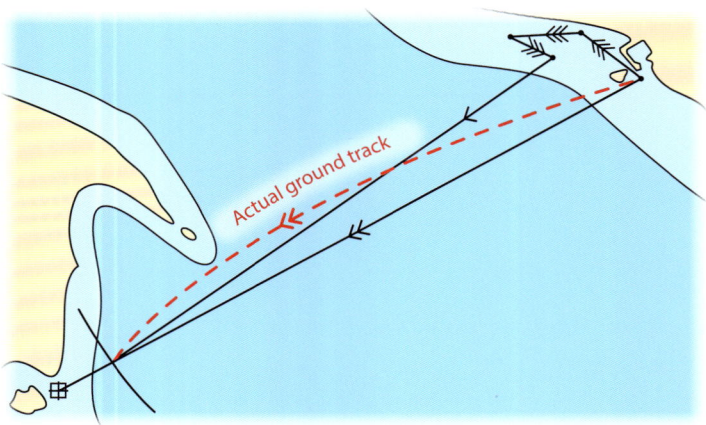

① Plot intended heading

② Add tidal vector

③ Gives EP and shows need to adjust initial heading

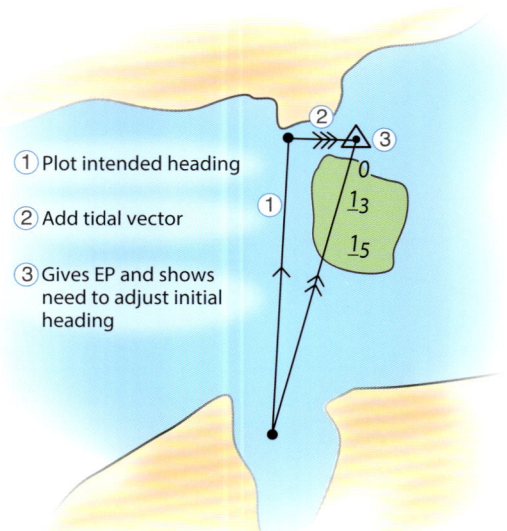

Projected Estimated Position

Before commencing the passage, use the Estimated Position technique to predict where the stream will take you.

If the ground track takes you too close to danger, revise the heading.

NAVIGATION 7

Leeway

Leeway is the effect of wind on a vessel pushing it away from its intended track. To compensate for leeway, alter course by 5° or 10°, depending on the wind strength and type of vessel.

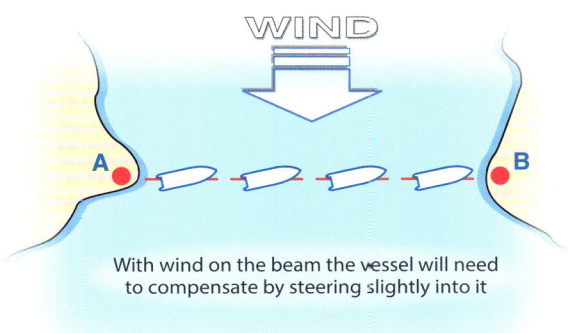

With wind on the beam the vessel will need to compensate by steering slightly into it

Chartwork Symbols

It is important when using a chart to get into the habit of using symbols that are universally understood.

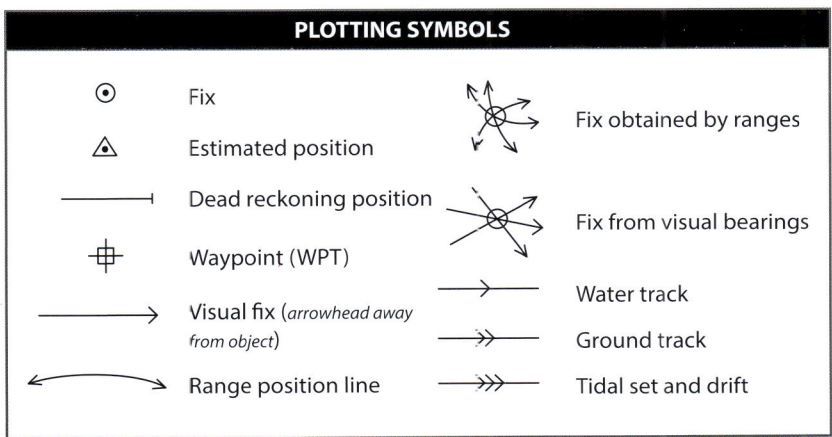

7 NAVIGATION

GNSS/Chartplotters

This chapter assumes an integrated approach to navigation is taken, choosing whichever techniques best suit the passage being made. GNSS/chartplotter units are a 'must fit' on almost all craft and are available to suit all budgets.

GNSS is in worldwide use and works by calculating a boat's position by reference to satellites orbiting the earth.

Chartplotters are available with buttons to control functions and settings, or as touchscreen versions with these same functions built into the screen/menus. Some sets combine these control methods.
By way of example, typical functions and controls include:

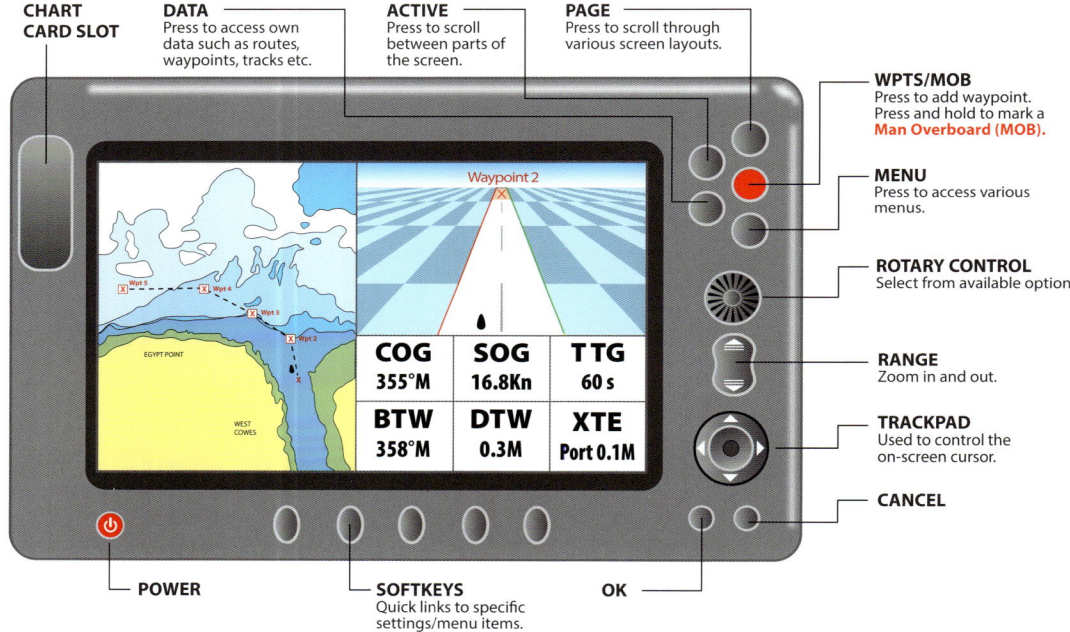

CHART CARD SLOT

DATA – Press to access own data such as routes, waypoints, tracks etc.

ACTIVE – Press to scroll between parts of the screen.

PAGE – Press to scroll through various screen layouts.

WPTS/MOB – Press to add waypoint. Press and hold to mark a **Man Overboard (MOB)**.

MENU – Press to access various menus.

ROTARY CONTROL – Select from available options

RANGE – Zoom in and out.

TRACKPAD – Used to control the on-screen cursor.

CANCEL

POWER

SOFTKEYS – Quick links to specific settings/menu items.

OK

COG – Course Over Ground – The track the vessel is heading down. May not be the direction the vessel is pointing (its heading) due to wind/stream.

SOG – Speed Over Ground – The speed the vessel is travelling over the surface of the earth. May be different to the speed through the water due to wind/stream.

BTW – Bearing to Waypoint – May be different to vessel heading due to wind/stream.

TTG – Time to Go – Time to run to waypoint.

DTG – Distance to Go – Distance to run to waypoint.

GOTO (in menu) – gives option to navigate directly to chosen waypoint. Units vary and some create a route from current position to destination waypoint whilst others don't. User must ensure route from current position to chosen waypoint remains safe.

MOB – when pressed indicates man overboard and bearing distance to marked position.

Cross Track Error (XTE or "Off Course") – distance off the direct route between two waypoints.

GNSS units that display position purely as latitude/longitude are available (and are a good back-up to have on board) but most have inbuilt charts and represent the vessel's position on them.

Which chartplotter you buy depends on the setup of a particular vessel. Laptops, tablet computers and phones can act as chartplotters but are best considered as back-ups, or as a planning aid, as they are rarely designed to operate in a marine environment. With some tablets/phones the inbuilt GNSS units seem not as effective or accurate as dedicated ones.

Screen size is often a limitation as you need to scroll in and out to see detail or the 'big picture' – large or split screens can make this easier. Carrying paper charts to use in conjunction with electronic charts is essential.

As mentioned on page 50, the limitations and accuracy of GNSS/chartplotters need to be properly understood to use them safely and to best effect.

Navigation Tools

A hand bearing compass is a key tool. Choose one that is easy to use and works effectively at night.

Choose plotting instruments that will work well on a small, fast-moving craft.

Use a hand-held GNSS for the waypoint web or compass rose waypoint techniques. It is always useful to have a back-up set anyway.

Small white and red torches are essential for chartwork at night.

7 NAVIGATION

Higher-speed Navigation

At higher speeds it is essential that you know where you are at all times as it is easy to run into danger very quickly.

The techniques used at higher speeds are the same as those used at lower speeds, but some methods will work far better than others. For example, in smaller boats in rougher conditions, plotting a latitude/longitude as a means to fix position is extremely challenging, whereas using the bearing to compass rose technique is highly effective and simple. Create plans using techniques that will work in the environment you will be boating in.

See also page 128.

Calculating Speed v. Time v. Distance

$$\text{Speed} = \frac{\text{Distance}}{\text{Time}} \quad \text{or Time} = \frac{\text{Distance}}{\text{Speed}}$$

If your speed is 15 knots how long will it take to travel three miles?

$$3 \text{ miles at } 15 \text{ knots} = \frac{3}{15} \text{ of an hour} = \frac{1}{5} \text{ of an hour} = 12 \text{ minutes}$$

Another method:

Fifteen knots is 15 nautical miles in 60 minutes, or 1.5 miles in six minutes (having divided both numbers by 10)

Therefore three nautical miles at 15 knots takes 12 minutes

NAVIGATION 7

Latitude and Longitude

As we know, horizontal and vertical gridlines on charts can precisely define our position anywhere in the world. North–south lines between the poles are meridians of longitude, east–west lines dividing the Earth into layers are parallels of latitude.

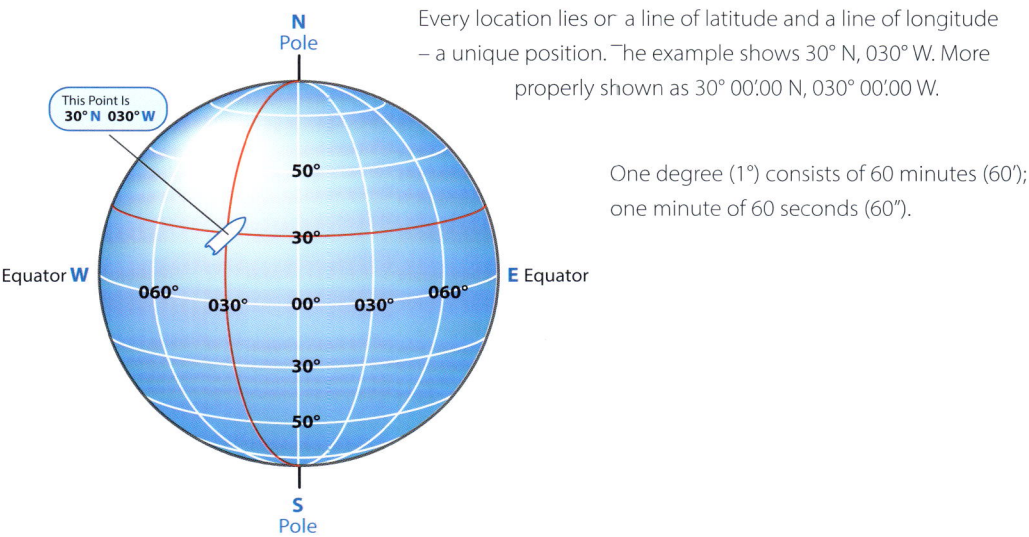

Every location lies on a line of latitude and a line of longitude – a unique position. The example shows 30° N, 030° W. More properly shown as 30° 00′.00 N, 030° 00′.00 W.

One degree (1°) consists of 60 minutes (60′); one minute of 60 seconds (60″).

Different Ways of Representing Latitude and Longitude

The way that latitude and longitude is represented has evolved.

Degrees, minutes and seconds	50° 50′ 30″ N, 001° 19′ 45″ W	Older nautical format, occasionally used
Degrees, minutes and decimals of a minute	50° 50′.50 N, 001° 19′.75 W	Currently used nautical format
Degrees and decimals of a degree	50.842° N, 1.329° W +50.842°, −1.329°	Common on smartphone/tablet apps

The simplest way to convert between formats is to use a website or app or use a GNSS/chartplotter to enter the position and then change the format.

To do so manually:

What is 50.842° N, 1.329° W in the currently preferred nautical xx° xx′.xx N, xxx° xx′.xx W format?

The '50' and '1' are the degrees, so transfer straight across as 50° xx′.xx N, 001° xx′.xx W

The '.842' and the '.329' is of a maximum of 60 minutes. Therefore, 0.842 x 60 = 50.52 and 0.329 x 60 = 19.74. So, when converted it is 50° 50′.52 N, 001° 19′.74 W. The small difference is due to rounding.

RYA ADVANCED POWERBOAT HANDBOOK

7 NAVIGATION

Horizontal Chart Datums

Paper charts show a code, often 'WGS84' (World Geodetic System 1984), which is the latest assumption of the position of the lines of latitude and longitude.

Some countries and older charts use different datums (e.g. 'OSGB36' on older UK charts, 'ED50' in Europe). The effect of different datums essentially slightly moves lines of latitude and longitude east–west and north–south.

This is important as GNSS units default to the WGS84 datum, so a chart position from one datum (e.g. OSGB36) used to enter a waypoint in a GNSS introduces an error. The error may range from a hundred metres to considerably more. At sea in open water this may not matter, but nearer to land it could be catastrophic.

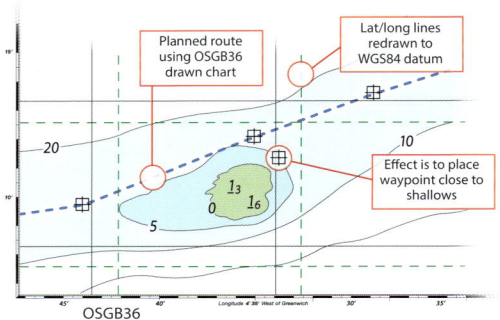

Charts

Charts vary in size and colours used and may be paper-based or electronic.

Potential Advantage/ Disadvantage	Paper-based	Electronic-based		
		Chartplotter	Laptop	Tablet/phone
Battery/electronics fail?	No	Yes	Yes	Yes
Can be difficult to see the 'big picture' and/or detail?	No – assuming correct sizes/scales	Depends on screen size. Split screen versions help	Depends on screen size	Depends on screen size
Charts go out of date?	Yes – updates on the internet	Yes – update the cartridge/card or by download	Yes – update the cartridge/card or by download	Yes – update by download
Designed for the marine environment?	Depends – waterproof charts available	Yes – except rear connectors	No – use in wheelhouse	No – but covers available
Position errors?	Always possible	Yes – must understand GNSS accuracy	Yes – must understand GNSS accuracy	Yes – must understand GNSS accuracy. GNSS unit may be less accurate
Charting errors?	Always possible but less likely	Always possible	Always possible	Always possible

68 RYA ADVANCED POWERBOAT HANDBOOK

NAVIGATION 7

Electronic Charts

Initially, electronic charts were effectively copies of paper charts with lines of latitude and longitude superimposed – raster charts. Full digital versions (vector charts) were then introduced, with layers of data that can be 'switched' off and on.

Harbour photos, seabed profiles etc. are available on some charts. Overloading the screen can confuse, though – sometimes 'less is more'.

Chart Techniques

Heading = the direction the vessel is pointing. Course = the direction the vessel is travelling (this may equal heading). Bearing = the direction from the vessel to another object.

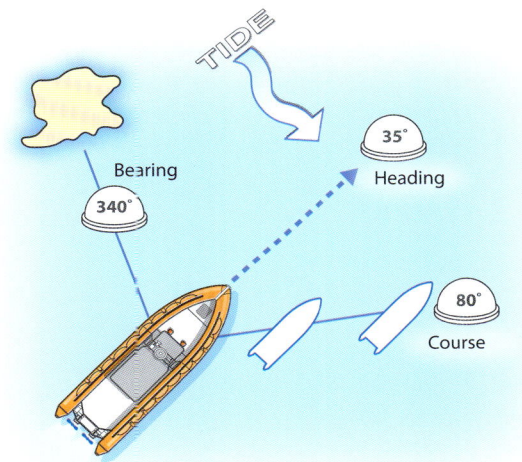

Range and Bearing: The plotting tool accurately measures the bearing between two positions. A simple solution is to slide the edge of your hand to the compass rose.

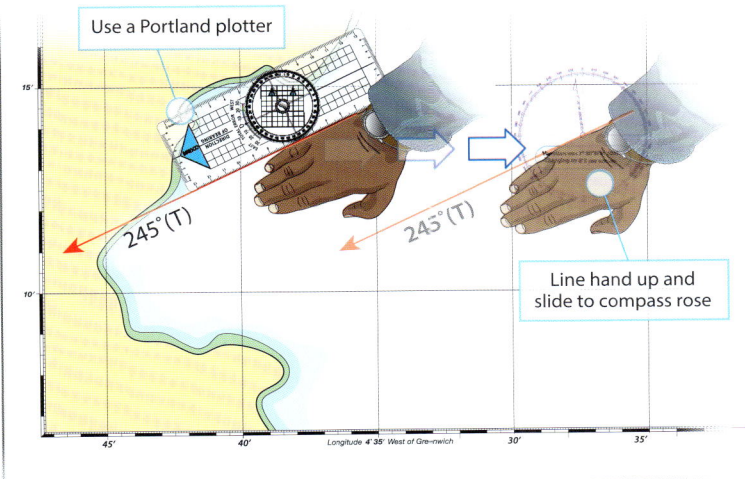

NAVIGATION

Measuring distance: Dividers are accurate (1' = 1 Nm), fingers are approximate.

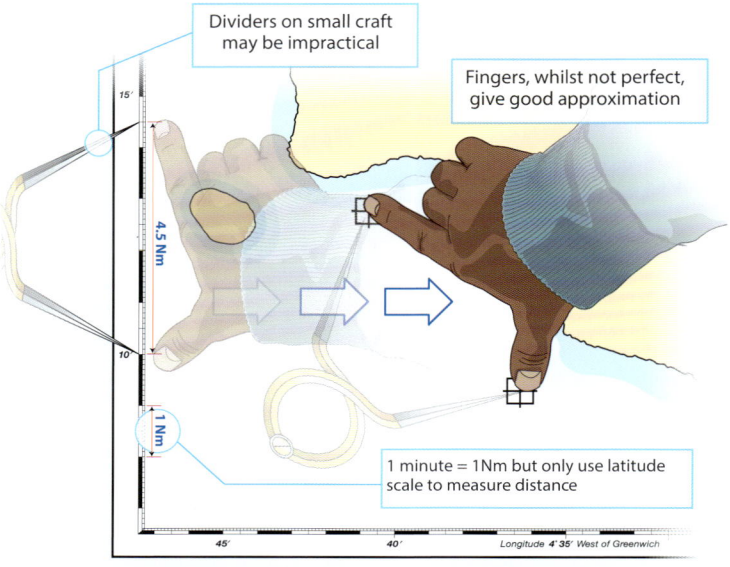

Dividers on small craft may be impractical

Fingers, whilst not perfect, give good approximation

1 minute = 1Nm but only use latitude scale to measure distance

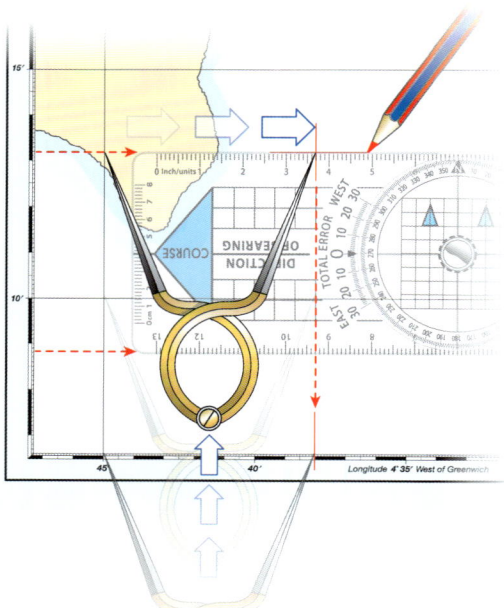

Plotting a position: Plot or read your position using dividers or a plotting tool. Keep the tool parallel to gridlines and transfer the position from the scale to the area of chart or from the position to the scale.

Dividers can be used too. Measure to a vertical or horizontal gridline.

Another solution is to use a sheet of paper lined up with the grid lines. When afloat, this could be a laminated piece of paper.

NAVIGATION 7

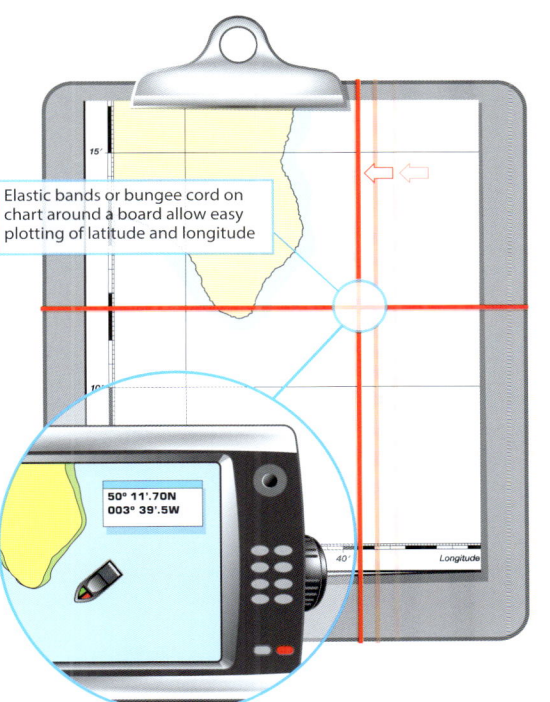

Elastic bands or bungee cord on chart around a board allow easy plotting of latitude and longitude

Another solution includes using bungee cords or elastic bands.

Slide the bands to line up with the required latitude and longitude.

Variation & Deviation

You will be aware how to identify the variation for the area that you are boating in, how to update it to its current figure and how to adjust the courses and bearings you take from a chart to account for the variation.

As an advanced powerboater boating in various locations, you should be able to assess quickly the impact of variation. Variation of 2° or 3° may be largely irrelevant on an open RIB where the steering compass is graduated with 5° intervals and you struggle to steer with greater than 10° accuracy. On another craft it may be more relevant, or in places where it may be 10°–15° it cannot be ignored.

As you will recollect, deviation is the error in a compass reading caused by the presence of ferrous items or electromagnetic fields near the compass. Additionally, mobile phones and handheld VHF radios placed near a compass may cause significant deviation.

If you use a variety of craft as a skipper, deviation may be non-existent on one craft but on another render the steering compass irrelevant unless you have a deviation card. Always check for deviation when helming a different craft for the first time so you know whether it is a problem or not before an issue arises.

Assess deviation using a hand bearing compass. Compare headings between the hand bearing and the main steering compass at 15° intervals. The difference is plotted on a deviation card. Alternatively, use the comparison with Course Over Ground from the GNSS/chartplotter at 15° intervals.

The introduction of new electronics or fittings may alter deviation, so a regular check is advisable.

RYA ADVANCED POWERBOAT HANDBOOK

7 | NAVIGATION

Tides and Tidal Streams

Tides may have a significant impact on your boating and arise from the interaction of the sun, moon and Earth.

Additionally, the height of tide is also influenced by weather. High atmospheric pressure 'pushes' the water level down; low pressure allows the water level to rise. As a rough guide, 34mb of pressure difference from the average for an area may affect tidal height by up to 0.3m.

As an advanced powerboater you need to be comfortable with the causes of tides, where to get tidal information and how it may impact your boating.

There is a wealth of tidal information available:

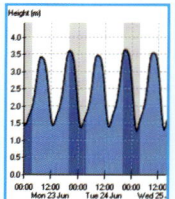 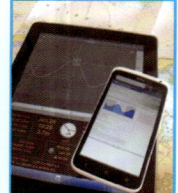 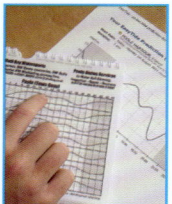 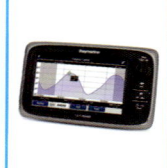 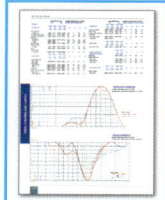

| Usually free on the internet within a seven-day period – charges may apply for a longer term | Plenty of apps are available for phones, tablets and computers | Local tidal booklets show tidal curves or data | Chartplotters usually show tidal curves and may show tidal stream too | Almanacs give times and heights of high and low water for major ports. Use the tidal curve to calculate tidal heights between these times |

When tidal height becomes critical it may be beneficial to cross-reference tidal heights between sources, as differences sometimes exist.

Understandably, there has been a shift towards obtaining tidal information from online and electronic sources. Be careful to ensure that you can still create a tidal curve from an almanac in case you ever need to. Likewise, whilst you may rarely need to undertake a secondary port calculation, ensure you are able to do so in case the need arises.

NAVIGATION 7

Rule of Twelfths

Techniques that allow you to get rough and ready results when afloat are always useful. The rule of twelfths is just such a technique and is one that merits practising so you are happy to use it when necessary. It can be used to give a rough indication of tidal heights between high and low water times.

0030	6.7m
0645	0.6m
1300	6.8m
1915	0.7m

The range is 6.1m. One-twelfth of 6.1m is about 0.5m. The rule of twelfths states:

- Hour 1: 1/12th of water moves = 0.5m
- Hour 2: 2/12th of water moves = 1.0m
- Hour 3: 3/12th of water moves = 1.5m
- Hour 4: 3/12th of water moves = 1.5m
- Hour 5: 2/12th of water moves = 1.0m
- Hour 6: 1/12th of water moves = 0.5m

Add or subtract as many hours of the tide as you need to from the high/low water height.

Tidal Terminology

It is important to remember the terminology surrounding tidal heights.

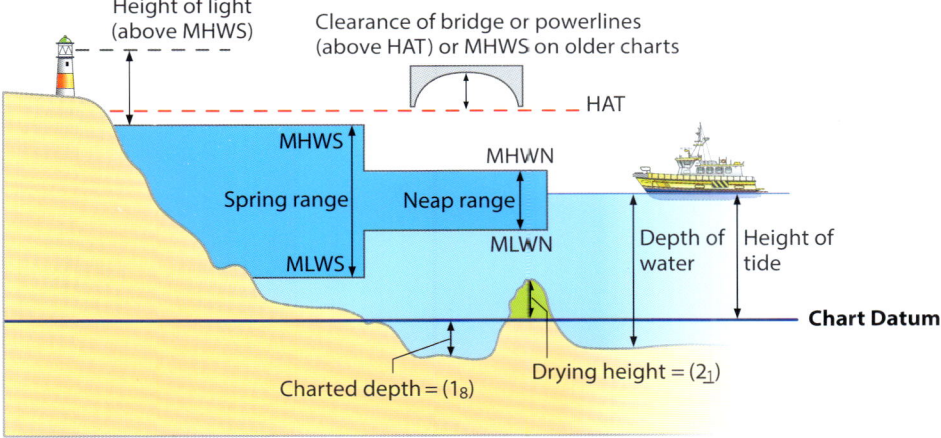

Highest Astronomical Tide (HAT)
Mean High Water Neaps (MHWN)
Mean High Water Springs (MHWS)
Mean Low Water Neaps (MLWN)
Mean Low Water Springs (MLWS)

Spring tides have the largest range. A larger range means there is more water to move between high and low water, so there is a faster flow. A spring range is typically two times that of a neap range.

Tip: A high-water spring tide will occur at roughly the same time each day.

7 NAVIGATION

Secondary Ports

While not often used in the days of apps on tablets and phones, tidal information on the internet etc., knowing how to calculate tidal heights at secondary ports remains a skill advanced powerboaters should develop.

This technique uses almanac data to create a tidal curve for smaller ports and harbours.

- From an almanac, note the data about the port/harbour and which standard port to use.
- Determine the time difference between high water (HW) at our secondary port and the standard port using the techniques detailed in the images.
- Adjust for Daylight Saving Time if needed and enter this adjusted HW time into the tidal curve for the standard port.
- Use the same techniques to adjust tidal heights for use in the tidal curve.

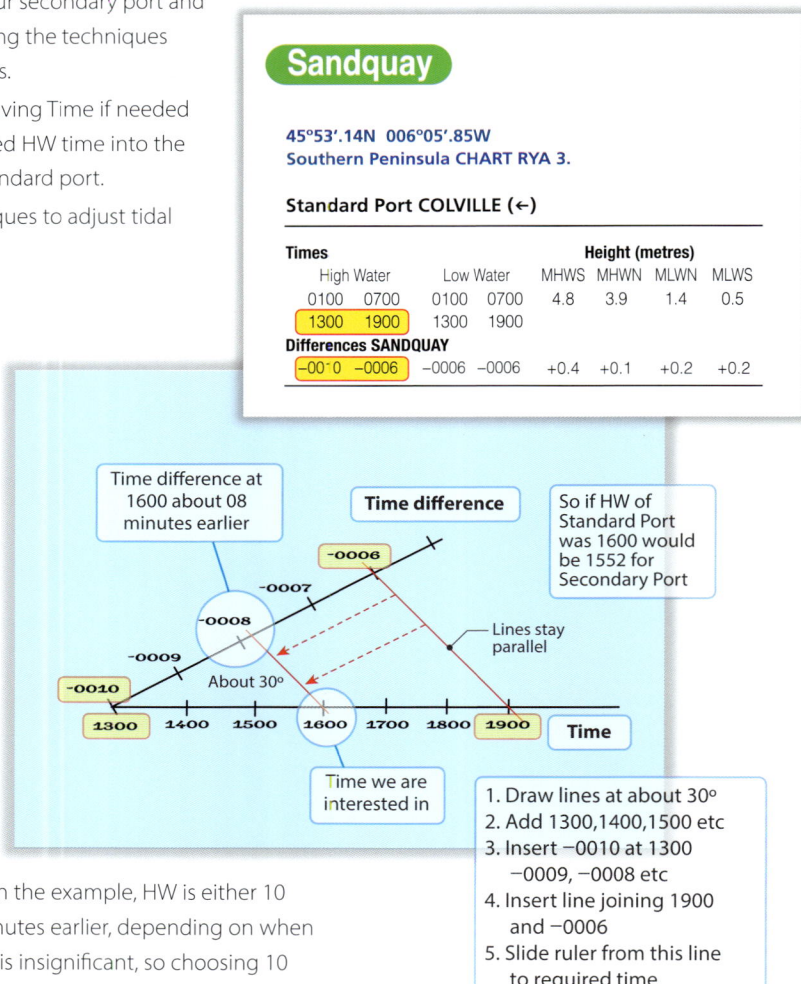

'Crocodile' technique

Keep it simple though. In the example, HW is either 10 (-0010) or six (-0006) minutes earlier, depending on when it occurs. The difference is insignificant, so choosing 10 minutes is a reasonable assumption.

Likewise, does tidal height difference matter? Assess each situation individually. Decide when to use a method or when an approximation will do.

NAVIGATION 7

The 'crocodile' technique for secondary ports works well for most people, but there is also the linear-scale method as an alternative.

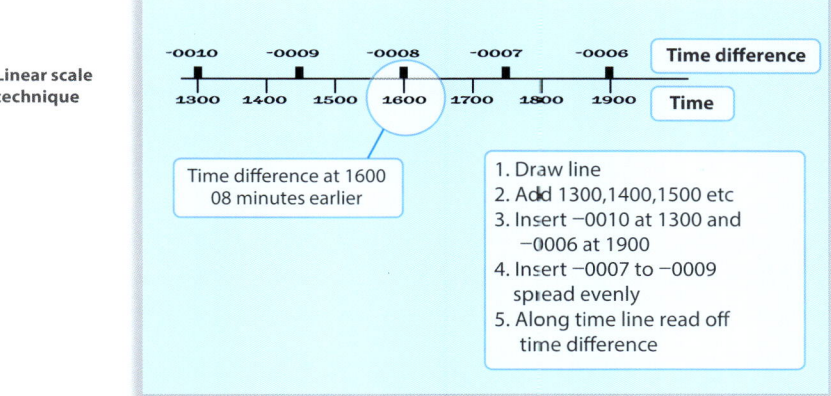

Linear scale technique

Tidal Streams

The rise and fall of tide may be influential if we get afloat at a launch site, need to navigate a channel or anchor safely at our destination. Flow of water (stream) has a significant bearing on us too, and can create dangerous conditions.

Flow rates on spring tides are typically about twice those of neap tides, as there is roughly twice the range.

Stream can affect us in various ways:

Tidal stream may slow us down or speed us up. At slow speed, a strong tide against us may reduce speed significantly and waste fuel. Equally, stream behind us might increase our Speed Over Ground and save fuel.

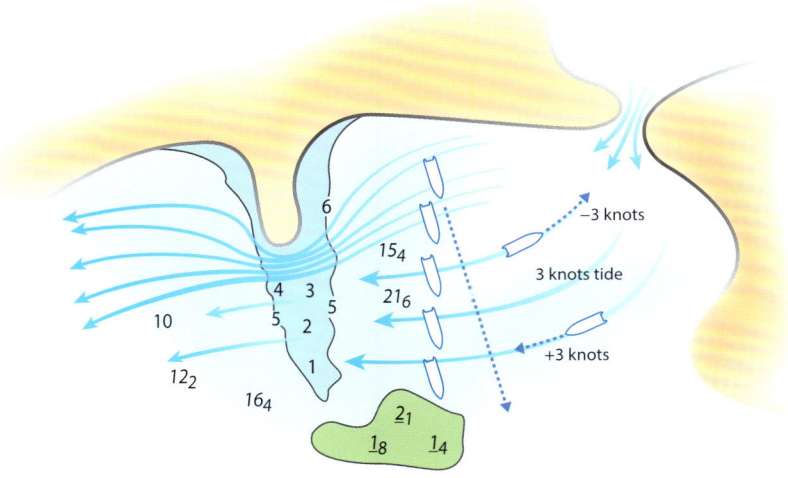

RYA ADVANCED POWERBOAT HANDBOOK

7 NAVIGATION

On our beam it may push us off course, which in some situations could lead us into danger.

Across a rough seabed in shallower water, stream creates disturbed water. If the wind is opposed to the stream, seas will be even rougher.

Through constrictions and around headlands the rate of flow will increase.

Tidal stream information is found from almanacs and charts.

Tidal stream information is often available on chartplotters but it may be difficult to use the tidal stream data from here to plan future passages.

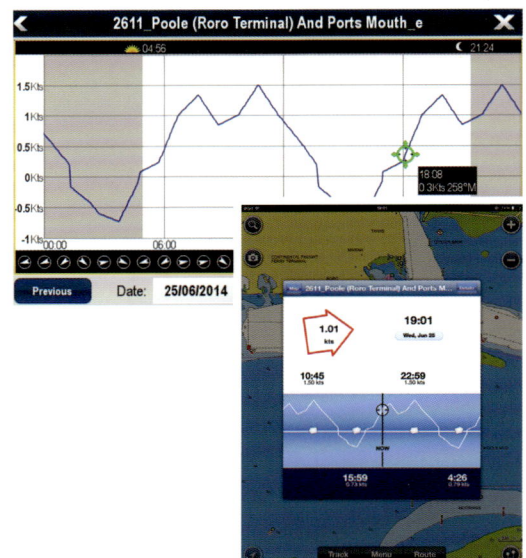

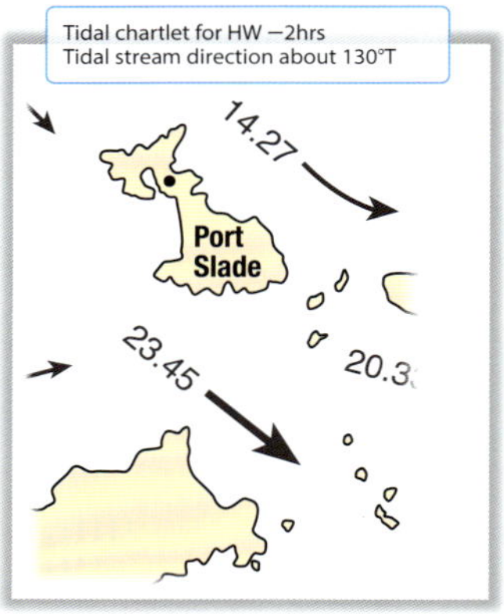

Tidal chartlet

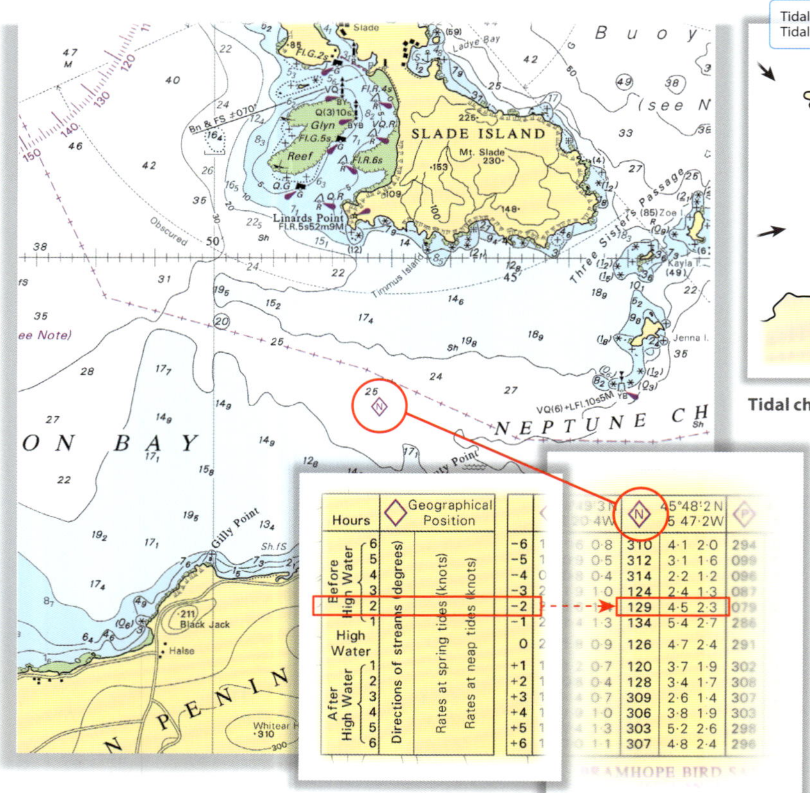

Tidal diamonds

76 RYA ADVANCED POWERBOAT HANDBOOK

NAVIGATION 7

Determine the high water time for the chart or diamond (the HW time may refer to a port a long distance away). Use data:

- To determine the rate and direction of flow at the time you envisage passing through an area.
- To choose a time (or range of times) when the rate is hindering or favourable to your passage – a 'tidal window' or 'tidal gate'.

It is the same area and the same time relative to high water for each image. The numbers are the same – 23.45 on a tidal stream chartlet means the rate is 2.3 knots at neaps 4.5 knots at springs.
On a chartlet, use a plotting tool to determine the direction.

The 'Tidal Hour'

Tidal rate and direction are only approximations and vary throughout the tidal cycle. The above example of 4.5 knots and 129°T represents the data at that point in time – HW minus two hours.

We assume that it applies consistently over that hour before it changes to 5.4 knots and 134°T at HW minus one hour.

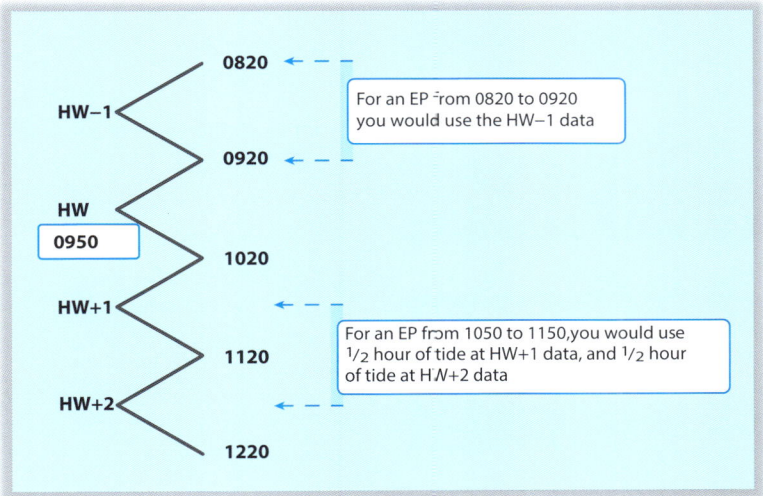

We can use the 'tidal hour' technique to create a greater degree of accuracy if we feel it useful. Drawing the 'zig-zag' lines and adding the timings in helps us to 'see' which tidal hours to use in calculations.

We will use this assumption when calculating estimated positions or course to steer.

Chapter 8

Radar and AIS

Radar offers many benefits – various ways to fix position, track other craft and determine whether a risk of collision exists, and a means to navigate close to land. An Automatic Identification System (AIS) offers an additional way to identify some other craft. Both are attractive options on smaller vessels.

Radar consists of two elements:

Antenna: The scanner is either encased in a 'radome' or visible ('open array'). Radomes are common on smaller craft.

Mount as high as possible with a clear view of the horizon.

The antenna rotates and sends out a signal (beam) which is reflected by targets. The quality of the return is determined by the size, material, texture, aspect and shape of the target.

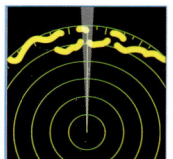 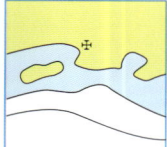 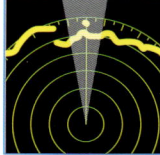

Bigger antennas deliver narrower beam width and better target discrimination.

Wider beam width stretches a target, making it seem larger. The disadvantages of a wider beam width may be that an entrance gets lost.

Display: Displays come in a variety of sizes – usually, the bigger the better. They may have touch-screen controls, physical buttons or a mixture. Some can be linked to tablet computers.

Tuning

Automatic tuning systems are usually very effective. However, manually adjusting settings may improve the quality of image. To obtain the best picture, frequently review and adjust settings.

Range: Adjusts how far away you are 'seeing'
Brilliance: Adjusts screen brightness
Gain: Like squelch on VHF – filters out some signals
Tune: Adjusts the frequency, which can vary with temperature changes
Rain and Sea Clutter: Can compensate for effects of rain or waves

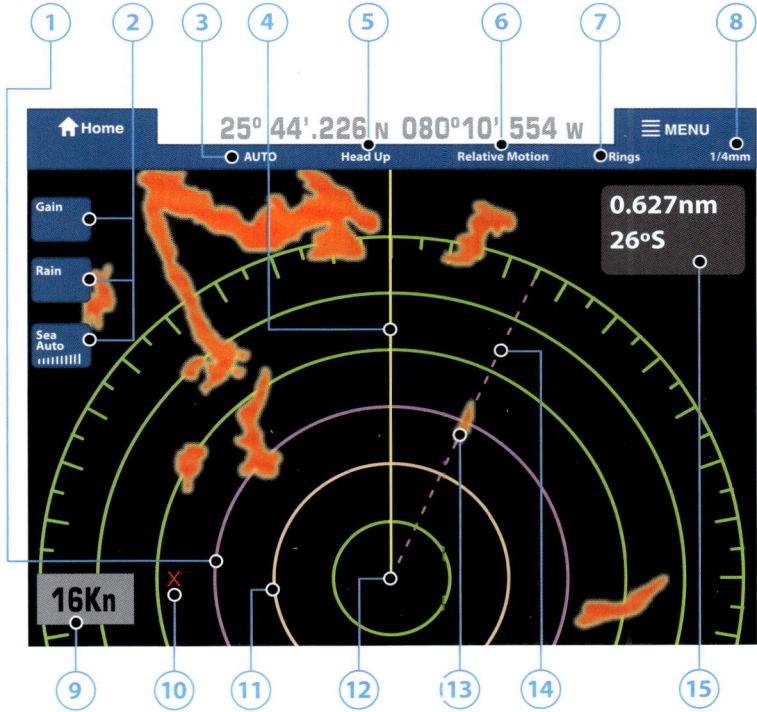

1. Variable Range Marker (VRM) is a ring that moves in/out to measure distance
2. On-screen tuning controls
3. Gain setting
4. Ship's Heading Marker (SHM)
5. Orientation mode (Head Up, North Up or Course Up)
6. Motion mode
7. Range rings off/on
8. Range ring spacing
9. Information overlay on screen
10. Waypoint
11. Safe zone ring
12. Ship's position
13. Target
14. Electronic Bearing Line (EBL is rotated onto target to measure) bearing. If target 'slides' along EBL towards vessel collision will probably occur
15. Target data – the bearing may be represented as a True/Magnetic bearing to the target (e.g. 124°M) or as a relative bearing to the heading of the vessel. For example 26°S means the target is 26° to the starboard of the vessel's present heading. A heading sensor is fitted as part of the radar installation.

8 RADAR AND AIS

Overlaying radar onto a chartplotter is useful as an indicator of any error in GNSS position or radar-heading alignment; i.e. if everything is working correctly the target for a navigational buoy will be directly on top of its charted position. If not, it may be a poor GNSS position or the radar display not showing the true heading. There can be a danger of information overload, so choose carefully the data to display.

Collision Avoidance

In poor or reduced visibility and at night, radar gives an early warning of other vessels, buoyage etc.

Mini Automatic Radar Plotting Aid (MARPA)

This tracks targets that are a possible collision risk, calculates course and speed and alerts you if a risk of collision exists. Tracking multiple targets is usually possible but you should still keep a very good lookout. MARPA relies on a steady and accurate heading. Therefore, it is worth monitoring accuracy during normal visibility before using it in poor visibility.

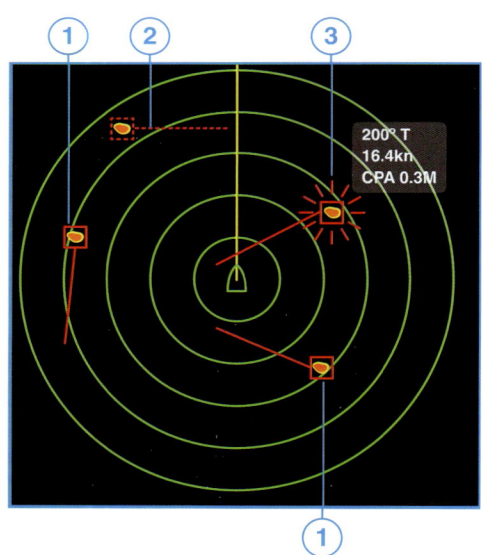

1. Safe target
2. Target being acquired
3. Dangerous target showing course and speed. Vector indicates likely Closest Point of Approach (CPA)

Navigation

Radar is a very effective aid to pilotage and a means to fix position. See Chapter 7 – Navigation.

Getting the most from radar requires a really good understanding of what it can do and particularly how to set it up to return the best results. Attending an RYA Radar course is strongly recommended.

RADAR AND AIS | 8

Radar Reflectors

SOLAS V requires that you carry and (if possible) fit a radar reflector.

Passive reflectors reflect a radar signal back to the sending antenna, giving more-effective return than the vessel alone would.

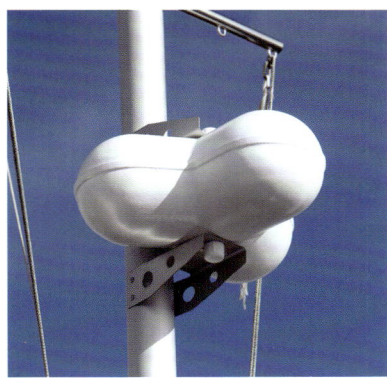

Active reflectors require a power source. They detect a radar beam and return an enhanced signal. Always fit a passive reflector too in case of a loss of power.

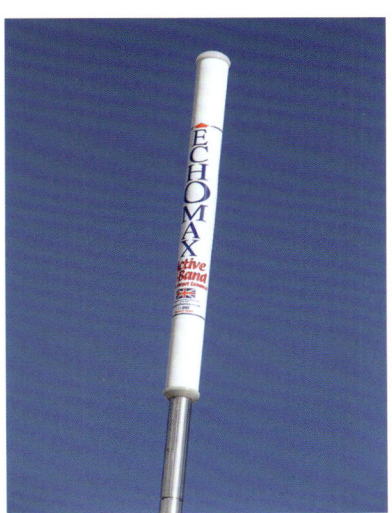

Automatic Identification System (AIS)

AIS is required on large vessels and some smaller commercial craft. The transmitter broadcasts a vessel's name, MMSI, location, course and speed. Vessels fitted with receivers 'see' the information on their chartplotter/radar screen or a dedicated unit.

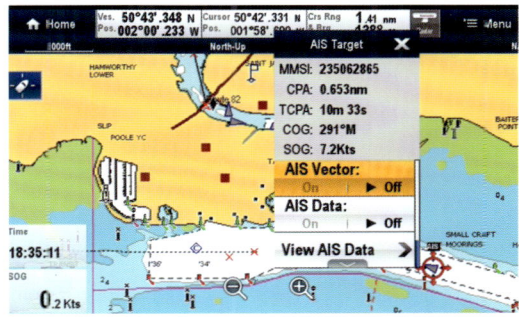

Smaller craft often fit AIS receivers or transmitters. Larger craft in busier areas may filter out transmissions, so do not assume your boat is being 'seen'.

AIS is not radar, as it only sees transmitting vessels. Craft may switch off their transmission or equipment failure may leave a vessel invisible to AIS.

Chapter 9

Weather

Whether to go to sea or to limit or change a passage in light of a forecast is often one of the most difficult and subjective decisions a skipper has to make.

Weather is a huge subject and every possible opportunity should be taken to enhance and develop knowledge, and understanding of how local factors interact with weather systems.

This chapter seeks to build on a level of existing understanding and focuses on how to use and interpret information.

An advanced powerboater should be able to:

- Understand weather systems
- Obtain forecasts of an appropriate type and detail for the passage being undertaken
- Interpret a synoptic chart
- Interpret forecasts and predict the impact on a passage
- Identify topography that may influence local conditions
- Decide whether to proceed, or adjust the plan

Forecasts

What type of forecast you need will vary according to the duration of a passage, the distance offshore, the type of vessel and the area that the passage is being undertaken in.

For close-to-shore, short-duration passages, a simple forecast may be enough.

Contains public sector information licensed under the Open Government Licence v3.0.

WEATHER 9

Up to 12 miles offshore, the inshore waters forecast is most relevant. Review the forecast for adjacent areas too.

A shipping forecast covers a very wide area and gives a good overview of the weather and likely changes. The General Synopsis gives an indication as to the presence, progression and development of weather systems.

These forecasts are available from various sources, e.g. VHF, internet, radio, but contain the same basic information. To be able to interpret an inshore or shipping forecast requires you to understand the meaning of words such as 'imminent', 'soon', 'later', 'rough', 'moderate' etc., which in the context of a forecast all have a very specific definition.

Cape Wrath to Rattray Head including Orkney

Strong winds are forecast
For coastal areas up to 12 miles offshore from 1200 UTC Sat 15 Sep until 1200 UTC Sun 16 Sep

24 hour forecast:
- **Wind** Southwesterly 5 to 7, occasionally gale 8 in north, decreasing 4 at times in Moray Firth.
- **Sea State** Slight or moderate in east, rough or very rough in north.
- **Weather** Occasional rain or showers.
- **Visibility** Moderate or good, occasionally poor in north.

Outlook for the following 24 hours:
- **Wind** Southwesterly 5 to 7.
- **Sea State** Slight or moderate in east, rough or very rough in north.
- **Weather** Showers.
- **Visibility** Good, occasionally moderate.

Low Iceland 983 expected Norwegian Sea by 0600 tomorrow. New low expected South East Iceland 982 by same time. High Fitzroy 1022 losing its identity by that time.

Select sea area: All Areas
Forecast type: Shipping Forecasts & Gale Warnings

Viking

Shipping Forecast - Issued: 1030 UTC Sat 15 Sep
- **Wind** Southwesterly 5 to 7
- **Sea State** Moderate or rough.
- **Weather** Rain or showers.
- **Visibility** Moderate or good.

North Utsire

Shipping Forecast - Issued: 1030 UTC Sat 15 Sep
- **Wind** Southwesterly 5 to 7
- **Sea State** Moderate or rough.
- **Weather** Rain or showers.
- **Visibility** Moderate or good.

For example, 'soon' refers to a weather system occurring in a period 6–12 hours from the time the forecast was issued. When considering a forecast it is easy to overlook the time of issue and fail to realise that a weather system that seemed 6–12 hours away may arrive in the next hour or two.

Remembering all of the definitions can be difficult. Learn the really important ones and know where to find the explanations of any you struggle to remember – an almanac is a good source.

A good tip is to create a portfolio of your preferred sources of weather information from the multitude available. Always compare forecasts from different sources, as rarely does all of the available information agree completely.

RYA ADVANCED POWERBOAT HANDBOOK

9 WEATHER

The Passage of a Depression (or Low)

As a reminder, the typical characteristics of a depression are:

- Unsettled weather
- Rainfall – often heavy
- Strong winds pointing towards the centre of the low (going clockwise in the Southern Hemisphere, anticlockwise in the Northern Hemisphere)
- Generally travelling west to east
- Closely spaced isobars, meaning stronger winds

Anticyclone (or High)

- Good settled weather
- Clear skies
- Light winds pointing away from the centre (going anticlockwise in the Southern Hemisphere, clockwise in the Northern Hemisphere)
- Widely spaced isobars

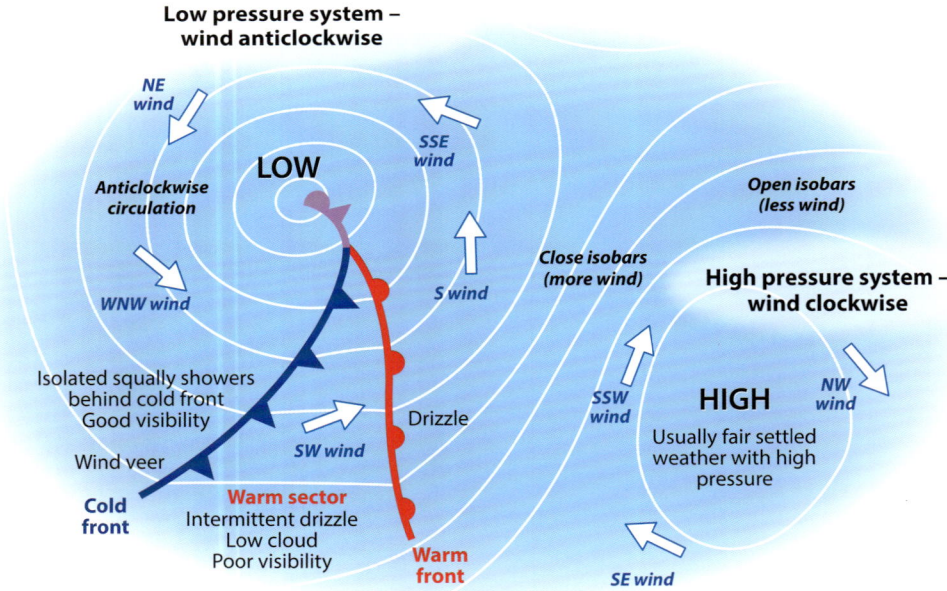

84　RYA ADVANCED POWERBOAT HANDBOOK

WEATHER 9

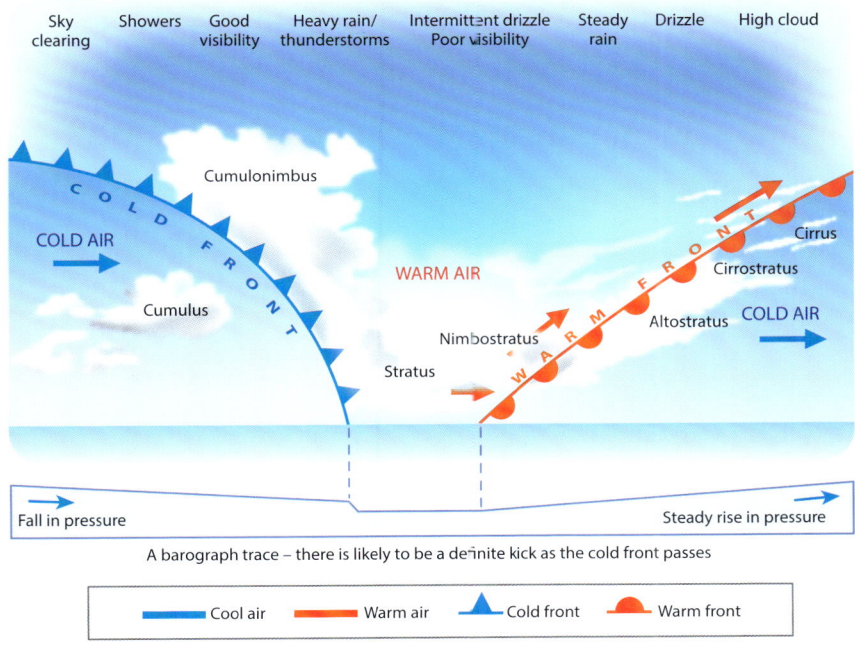

A barograph trace – there is likely to be a definite kick as the cold front passes

The Beaufort Scale

This was created to provide a link between wind strength and the sea conditions likely to be experienced afloat. As a more experienced boater you should have a good understanding of what wind speeds relate to the 'force' and what potential wave heights are likely to be experienced. Again, an almanac will always provide this information if you forget. See Chapter 15 – Wave Theory.

Fog

Avoid if possible as there is a real danger of a collision with another craft. Other vessels can be difficult to pinpoint and may be disorientated.

Sound the required signals and remember the rules change with respect to the actions vessels should take when not in sight of each other. See Chapter 6 – Collision Regulations.

The main types of fog are:

Radiation:
- Caused by rapidly cooling land where a warm, moist airstream exists
- Tends to occur overnight
- Disperses as the sun rises and heats land
- Common in autumn and winter

Advection (or sea fog):
- Caused by warm, moist air passing over cold water
- Higher winds (F4/F5) or a drier airstream will clear it
- Common in late spring and early summer

9 WEATHER

Synoptic Charts

Learn to read synoptic charts by comparing forecasts to them and developing the ability to create a mental picture of a synoptic from shipping and inshore forecasts, and vice-versa.

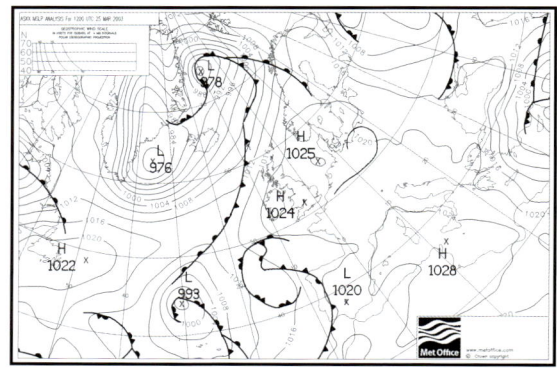

Weather Effects Influenced by Land

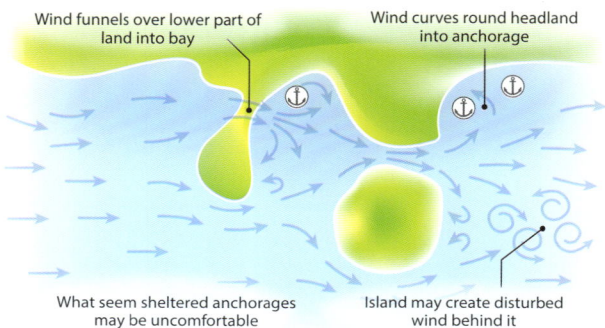

Sea Breeze

Sea breezes are common in spring and early summer. The wind strength rises from late morning into the afternoon. It blows at about 25° to the shoreline and can extend to about 15 miles offshore.

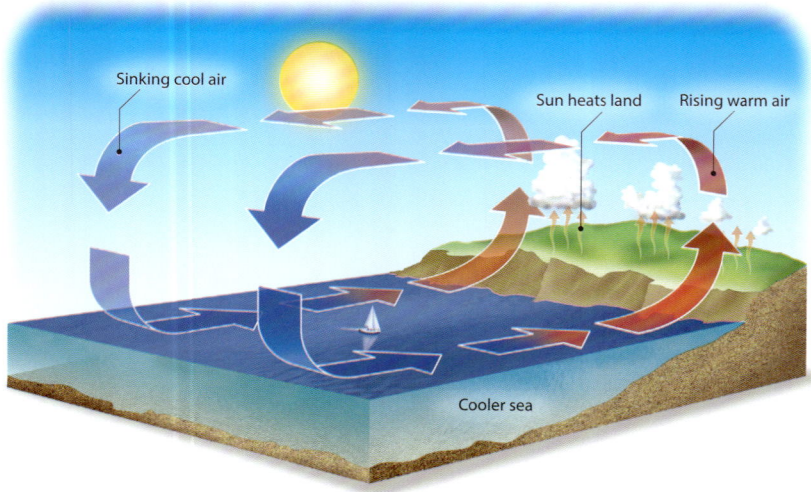

Land Breeze

These winds are gentler than sea breezes. They occur at night.

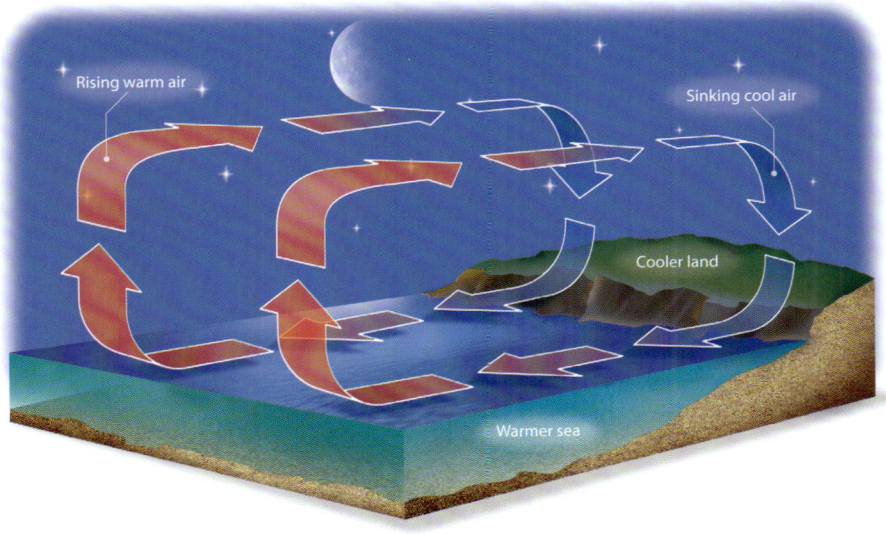

Katabatic Wind

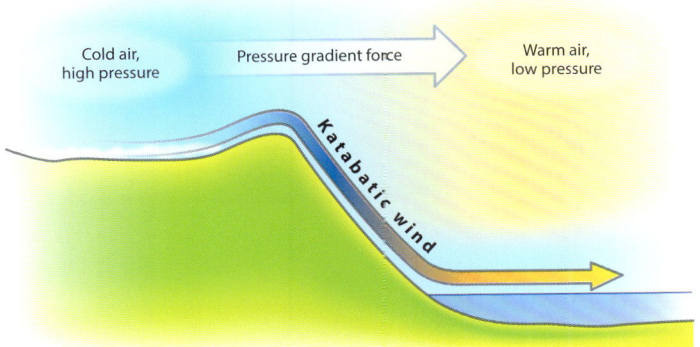

Chapter 10

Emergency Situations and Man Overboard

In the event of an incident afloat a good skipper will react calmly, assess the situation and decide on the best course of action. If it relates to another craft they will balance the safety of their crew and craft with the needs of the vessel requiring assistance.

There are many things that can go wrong on a vessel when at sea. Being able to deal effectively with them, whether on your craft or another vessel, will depend on training, practice and having the right equipment on board. Some common and serious issues include:

Water ingress: Understand where water can enter a vessel and have a plan to deal with each eventuality. For inboards, attach bungs of the correct size to each seacock, carry a kit to fix water pipes and learn how seawater flows from the intakes around the engine. Ensure bilge bumps work, strum boxes are clear and seacocks are checked. Consider carrying a spare bilge pump with hose and power leads attached that can be used to pump out another vessel.

EMERGENCY SITUATIONS AND MAN OVERBOARD | 10

Hull, porthole or tube damage: Carry blanking plates and tube repair kits. Where possible, know what materials you would use on a vessel to plug a larger hole in the event of a hull impact.

Fire: Ensure suitable extinguishers are carried and positioned correctly. Know how to deploy them. For inboards, make sure the engine fire system is operable and ensure you understand whether it is connected to an automatic engine shutdown system or whether there is a need to close air intakes. Mark battery and fuel switches and brief the crew on the switch locations and the need to turn them off in the event of fire.

Fuel: Don't run out! Know how to change and clear filters and, in the case of diesel systems, how to prime the fuel system. Carry plenty of spare filters.

Overheating: Be aware of the usual causes and perhaps create a checklist to help track a problem. Be able to change impellers on inboards and carry spares.

Attending courses on engine maintenance and fire-fighting can prove a good investment.

Man Overboard (MOB)

A person overboard from a vessel anywhere (irrespective of sea temperatures) is potentially a life-threatening situation. Rapid and efficient recovery is essential. The need to prevent an MOB occurring and the ability to deal with an incident if it occurs is key.

Causes and Prevention

Incidents can occur at slow and high speeds and be life-threatening. Causes include failure to hold on/sit down as a craft pulls away or accelerates; engaging astern with crew on the bow when berthing; overly aggressive driving; sudden shifts in direction, and failure to adopt a safe speed according to the sea state.

All are failures by the skipper to manage the people on their craft assertively and adapt their driving to the risks and conditions.

The very best way to deal with a man overboard is to ensure one never happens!

Preparing for it

What you wear and the safety kit you carry will depend on what you are doing afloat. Refer to Chapter 11.

Reset the track feature on the GNSS/chartplotter each trip so you can retrace your route if necessary.

Give a detailed safety briefing covering how to deploy and use the lifesaving appliances on board.

Practise all aspects of MOB situations (by day and night) on a regular basis, but don't risk putting live casualties in the water.

10 EMERGENCY SITUATIONS AND MAN OVERBOARD

Dealing with it

When an MOB occurs the training and drills should kick into action immediately:

- Loud shout of 'man overboard'. A crew member should point at the MOB and not stop until the crew has 'hands on' as it is easy to lose the casualty amongst the waves.
- Slow down in a straight line and turn back towards the casualty.
- Press the MOB button on the GNSS/chartplotter – it may help in locating the casualty.
- Are they conscious? Do they have a lifejacket on? Are they in any additional immediate danger? Assess the wind and determine the direction of approach. Will the stream carry them and the boat into danger during the recovery?
- If possible, deploy a lifebuoy. Even with a lifejacket on extra buoyancy may help/comfort them.
- Issue a DSC Distress alert and voice mayday call. It is better to stand-down rescue assets than launch them to a far more serious situation later. You can never be 100 per cent sure it will go perfectly.

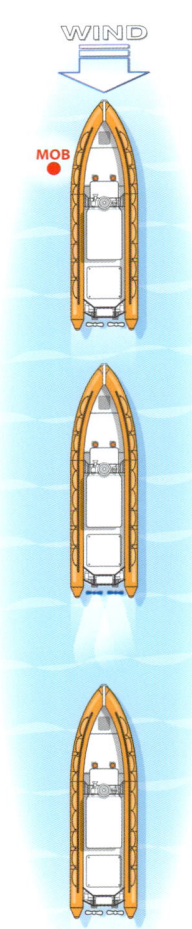

Method 1 – Into the Wind

- Start directly downwind at an appropriate distance to give time to settle the craft.
- Move slowly towards the MOB. Use neutral to limit momentum. The craft should be stopped short and just require a final nudge to reach them.
- Aim for the MOB to arrive on whichever side works best, depending on the boat layout. The crew should have a boathook and throw lines to hand.
- Grab the MOB and switch off the engine.* Secure a line to them if recovery into the craft will not be immediate. Move them to the best recovery position.

This method works best if there are crew present to grab the MOB.

*Safety point: An experienced, competent helm with crew may decide to keep the engine switched on when they consider it safer to do so in the light of sea conditions, hazards in the recovery area etc. This is a judgement for the skipper. Always switch off where possible.

90 RYA ADVANCED POWERBOAT HANDBOOK

EMERGENCY SITUATIONS AND MAN OVERBOARD 10

Advantages:	Disadvantages:
• Suits smaller craft with low freeboard and good access forward	• A misjudged approach could lead to the MOB going under the bow, with a real danger of injury in rougher conditions
• Allows waves to be taken head-on	• A higher bow limits the ability to see the MOB over the final few metres
• When rough, it may be preferable to being side-on to waves	• The helm needs to drive the craft until the final moment of 'contact'

Method 2 – Beam-on Approach

- Drive upwind of the MOB.
- Position the craft side-on to the waves.
- Aim at a point between half and two boat lengths upwind. Limit use of forward and reverse. Hold the craft beam-on to the waves and the MOB. Position the craft for the crew to grab them at an appropriate part of the vessel.
- Switch off the engine at the point of contact.*

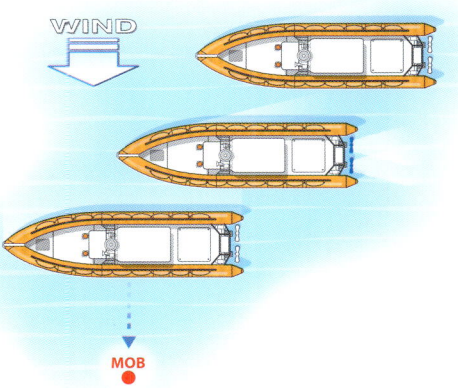

Advantages:	Disadvantages:
• Suits high-bowed vessels with limited forward access	• Being beam-on to waves can be uncomfortable and, in large breaking seas, dangerous
• Greater target/collection area – the whole of the side of the craft	• Smaller craft can be blown over the MOB
• Provides some shelter to the MOB	
• Once in position directly upwind, the craft does not need much helming, allowing use of VHF, preparation of recovery equipment etc.	

*Safety point: An experienced, competent helm with crew may decide to keep the engine switched on when they consider it safer to do so in the light of sea conditions, hazards in the recovery area etc. This is a judgement for the skipper. Always switch off where possible.

10 EMERGENCY SITUATIONS AND MAN OVERBOARD

The Williamson Turn

If sight of the MOB is lost at night or in restricted visibility, this method can be used to return along the vessel's own wake.

Recovery of the Casualty

Methods of recovering a person vary according to the craft and should be practised regularly.

Consider carrying dedicated MOB recovery equipment in craft that may be more likely to attend an MOB incident or suffer one themselves.

Casualty Aftercare

Contact rescue services immediately for detailed medical advice. Undertake a first aid course that focuses on water-related incidents.

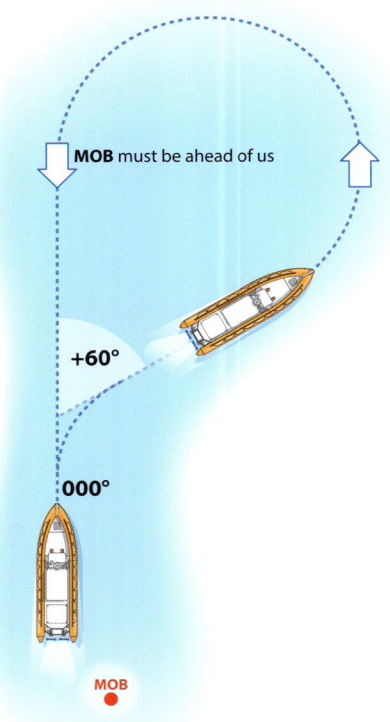

Note the heading and turn to starboard, adding 60° to the compass heading. Turn to port onto the reciprocal of the initial heading. The MOB should be ahead of you.

92 RYA ADVANCED POWERBOAT HANDBOOK

Chapter 11

Lifesaving Equipment

Your boat, you and your crew must be properly equipped with appropriate safety kit, be trained and experienced in its use and regularly practise deploying it. Passengers on board must be briefed to a suitable level.

Personal Kit

Commonly used equipment includes:

- Mini EPIRBs (Emergency Position Indicating Radio Beacon – also known as PLBs (Personal Locator Beacons)). These signal distress and location. The GNSS version is very accurate and preferable.
- Personal AIS beacons. They are based on the Automatic Identification System. An alert appears on the chartplotters of other AIS-enabled vessels.
- Handheld VHFs. Some have built-in GNSS and are DSC enabled.
- Locator beacons. Some sound an alarm on the chartplotter when the beacon is a certain distance from the vessel, others send alerts to a call centre.
- Personal flares. A combined day/night flare or perhaps a small set of rockets can be carried in a pouch.
- Strobe light/torch. It is essential to have a light in your lifejacket but an additional torch/light can be beneficial.
- Mobile phone in a waterproof pouch. A handy back-up.

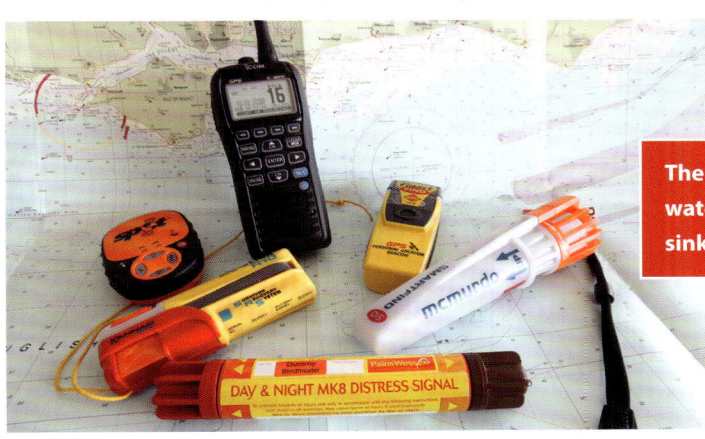

The ability to issue distress from the water in the event of an MOB or a sinking can be a lifesaver.

11 LIFESAVING EQUIPMENT

Boat Equipment

Equipment levels depend on the nature of operation. Perform a kit check before going afloat.

All equipment must be well stowed and secured in rougher conditions.

EPIRBs: GNSS versions give very accurate positions and are preferable.

AIS SARTs (Search and Rescue Transponders): These plot an alert onto the chartplotters of other AIS-enabled vessels.

Radar SARTs: A distinctive signal appears on all vessels with radar within 8–12 miles. They are more common on larger vessels.

Liferafts

Liferafts are required on commercial vessels and are a sensible addition to other vessels going further offshore or in remote locations. An RYA Sea Survival course ensures you know how and when to deploy it and how to survive in it.

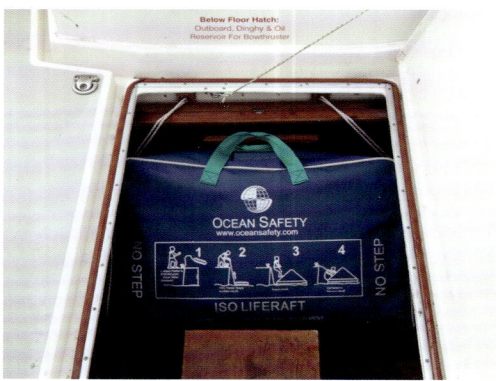

Stored in a locker in the cockpit, it must be easily accessible.

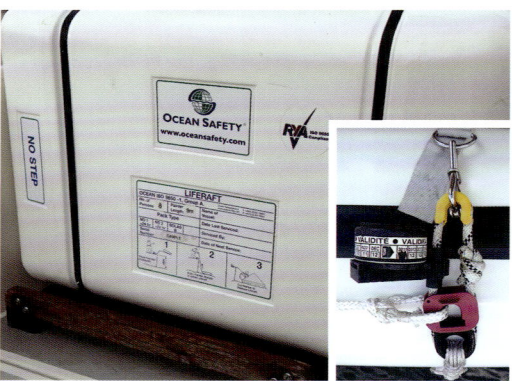

Here it is stowed on deck or the wheelhouse roof in a dedicated cradle. An automatic release system can be fitted to allow it to float free.

More effective electronic means of issuing distress make it less likely survivors will need to spend a long time in a liferaft before rescue.

Chapter 12

Searching and Search Patterns

The greater the time that you spend at sea, often in less favourable conditions, the greater the likelihood of being involved in an incident where you need to assist in a search.

Always be ready to receive and record a distress message. Responding to a distress or a request to assist with an incident is a requirement under SOLAS V but don't risk your crew and vessel – know your limitations and capability.

Always request assistance early and report a distress message or an MOB incident to the rescue services before commencing a rescue or search.

Incidents are controlled by Maritime Rescue Co-ordination Centres (MRCCs). You may act as their 'eyes and ears' and assist as appropriate.

This chapter introduces some of the techniques and terminology used when undertaking or assisting with a search but does not attempt to provide an exhaustive guide to search methodology.

12 SEARCHING AND SEARCH PATTERNS

Area v. Datum Searches

Datum searches are water-based.

- The area covered moves as the search vessel and casualty are affected by stream or wind.
- They rely on there being a good initial 'datum' – a distinct start point for the search.
- Only use the steering compass for heading. Do not use COG (from GNSS/chartplotter) or pick a point on the shore to steer to, as the search is a 'water search' and the search area must be allowed to move due to stream/wind.
- An expanding square search heads away from the datum whereas a sector search continually passes through the centre of the search area.

Area searches are ground-based. They cover a defined area and ignore stream and wind. They do not require a start point but cover an area.

Which search you undertake will be determined by:

- Confidence in initial datum.
- How long ago the casualty was reported missing.

To increase the probability of detection and best calculate the most likely location of the casualty, MRCCs use computer programs to calculate the search area.

The drift start point is where the MRCC starts its calculation.

Stream is added, followed by the effect of wind-driven current.

Finally, leeway is added and may vary greatly between 'types' of casualty. Therefore there can be large errors – 'divergence'.

From these three datums an area to search is calculated.

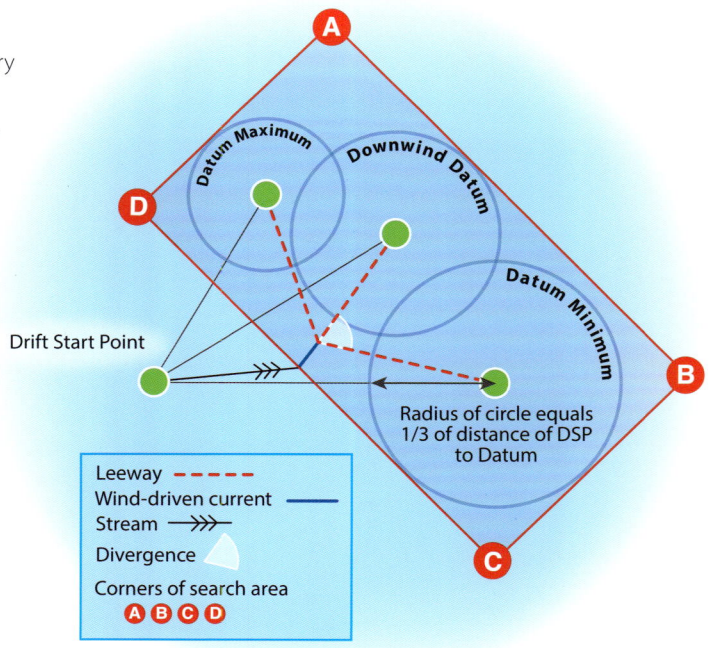

SEARCHING AND SEARCH PATTERNS 12

Track Spacing and Sweep Width

Sweep width should be the distance either side of the vessel the casualty can be expected to be spotted.

Track spacing is equal to sweep width.

For simplicity, track spacing should be taken as a maximum of 30 seconds for smaller craft searching for a person in the water in all sea states. Speed should be constant and appropriate to conditions.

Area Searches

Tips for area searches:

- Enter the corners of search area (A-B-C-D) as waypoints. Create a 'route' to show search area on chartplotter screen.
- The 'Course Over Ground' feature on a GNSS/chartplotter can be used for heading, as the search is a 'ground search'.

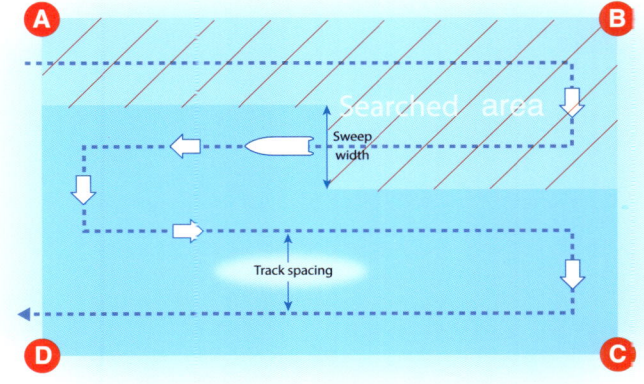

Parallel Track Search. The longest leg of the search is parallel to the longest leg of the search area

Things to consider when choosing a parallel track or a creeping line ahead search:

- The position of the sun (it's better to look away from it) or moon (it's better to look into it).
- Heading into wind may be uncomfortable but it allows good views abeam along wave troughs and crests. Heading at 90° to the wind may create an easier ride but it reduces the ability to see up/downwind when in troughs.
- Which end of the search area the search commences from is typically dependent on the approach course of the vessel.
- Where the casualty will most likely be in the search area may influence where to commence the search, as Creeping Line Ahead searches focus initially at one end of the search area.

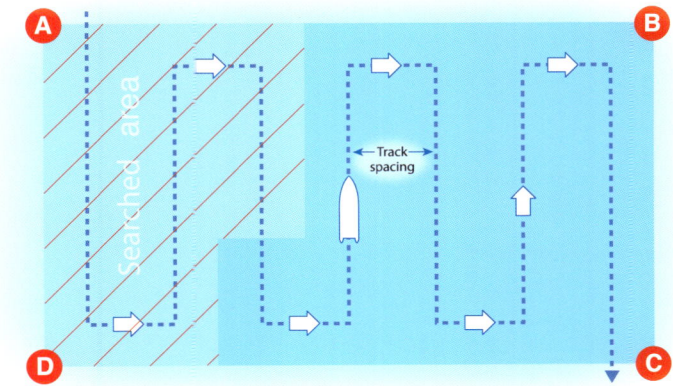

Creeping Line Ahead Search

RYA ADVANCED POWERBOAT HANDBOOK

12 SEARCHING AND SEARCH PATTERNS

Datum Searches

Initial heading of N, E, S or W for simplicity, ideally in the probable direction of the casualty.

In practice, because a datum search moves with the stream, if viewed on a chartplotter the pattern will be elongated in the direction of the stream.

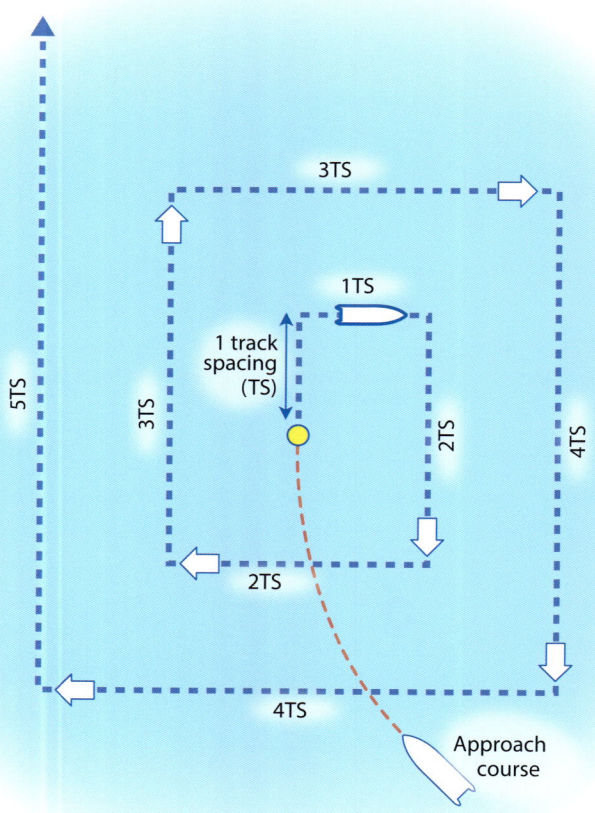

Expanding Square Search

SEARCHING AND SEARCH PATTERNS 12

The 'datum' is a target placed in the water and allowed to drift.

A sector search is shown for completeness. They are generally considered too complex for crew to execute.

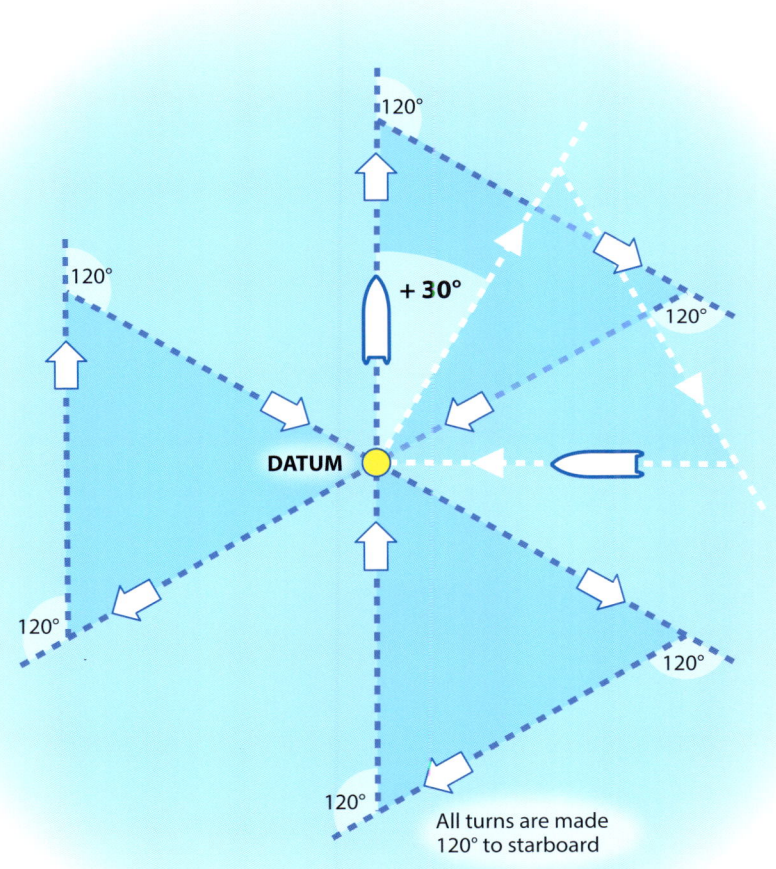

Sector Search

12 SEARCHING AND SEARCH PATTERNS

Other Searches

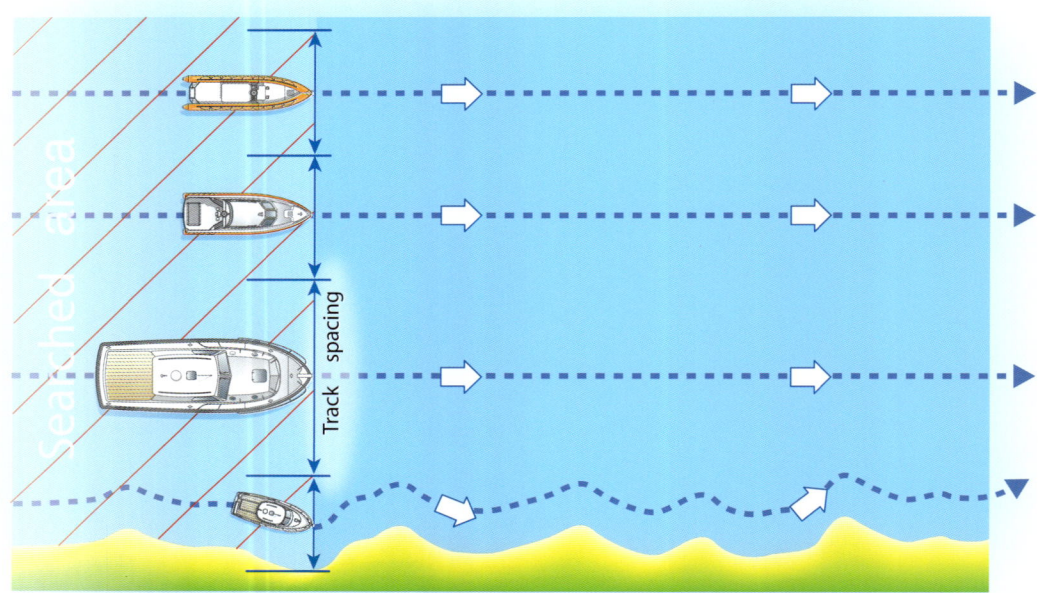

Multiple Vessels Search. Be careful to ensure the track spacing is appropriate for smaller craft

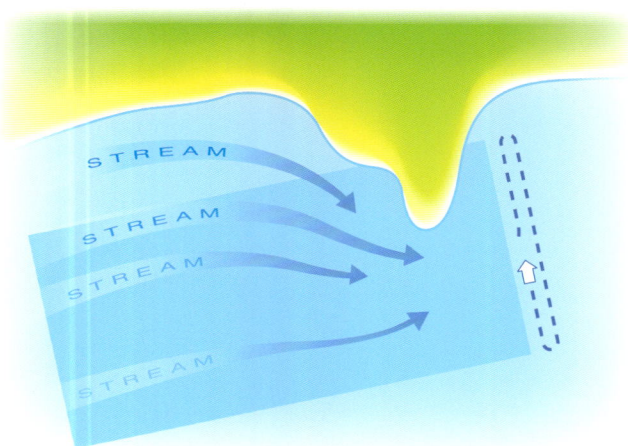

'Goalkeeper' Type Search. Wait at the exit of a search area for a casualty

SEARCHING AND SEARCH PATTERNS 12

Tips for undertaking a search:

- Clear old 'tracks' from the chartplotter. Start a new track to record the area searched.
- The helm steers the course or times the legs. The crew focus on lookout – vary positions during long searches.
- The boat speed throughout the search should be consistent.
- If deviation from the search pattern occurs (perhaps to check a possible sighting), ensure you return to the previous point. Don't create 'holes' in the search area – the track function on the chartplotter helps.

Never forget the obvious – a casualty will try to swim to shore or a moored boat if they are near enough, or could be holding on to a mooring buoy.

Tip: When initially recording incident details, if a specific lat/long position is given, the quickest way to enter into a chartplotter may be to scroll cursor N–S and E–W to position then use the 'goto' cursor.

Chapter 13

Rescue by Helicopter

If a casualty requires emergency evacuation the quickest method is usually by helicopter. Procedures vary from country to country and may also depend on the type of helicopter.

RESCUE BY HELICOPTER | 13

Before a lift, craft and crew must be prepared:
- Wear lifejackets. 'Spare' crew should be inside/below, if possible.
- Stow or secure loose gear.
- Delegate tasks and give a detailed brief before the noise of the helicopter makes this impossible.

The helicopter will establish contact on VHF Channel 16 or a working channel. They will decide whether they wish the vessel to be static (typical on RIBs and other small craft) or moving (typical on larger powerboats with deck areas where the winch person can be landed).

With professional crews that have undergone training, a pilot's preference will usually be to undertake a moving transfer, even on smaller vessels.

There are two types of transfer.

Vertical Transfer – Moving or Static

Winch person to be placed directly on deck – the vessel may be static or moving.

If it is a moving transfer, the helicopter will determine the speed and heading – usually either directly head to wind or 10°–20° off the wind at 5–15 knots. The helm must ensure there is sufficient searoom and suitable depth on the requested heading.

The winch person is lowered and may allow a short earthline hanging below to earth in the sea or on the boat before landing on deck and unclipping.

The winch person assumes responsibility, requests additional kit if required (e.g. a stretcher), assesses the casualty and co-ordinates extraction. Follow the winch person's instructions.

13 RESCUE BY HELICOPTER

Heaving-in Line ('Hi-Line') – Moving or Static

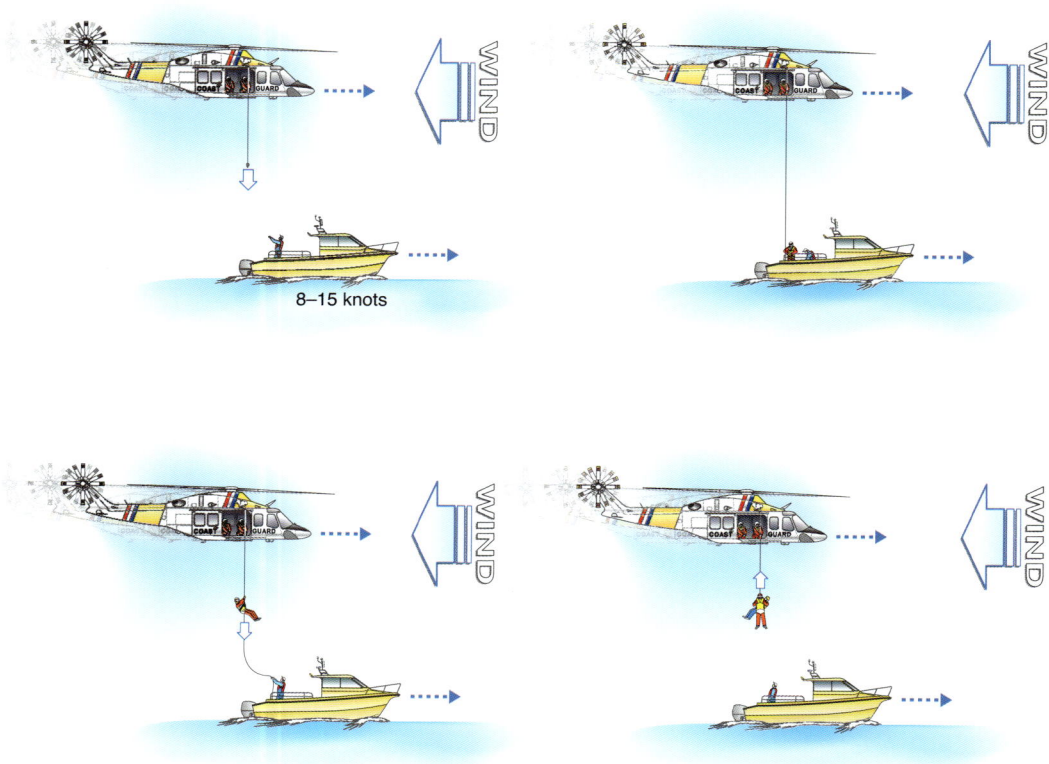

This is used when obstructions, a lack of deck area or difficulty in seeing the vessel prevents a vertical lift. The vessel may be static or moving.

Winch person lowers a weighted bag. When it is on deck, the helicopter moves off to one side and the winch person descends. The line is pulled by the boat's crew to ease the winch person into the boat. As with a direct vertical transfer, below the winch person will be an earthing line.

Never tie off the line to the vessel. Ideally coil it into a bucket – do not let it snag. Wear gloves.

The winch person takes charge and co-ordinates extraction as per vertical transfer.

RESCUE BY HELICOPTER | 13

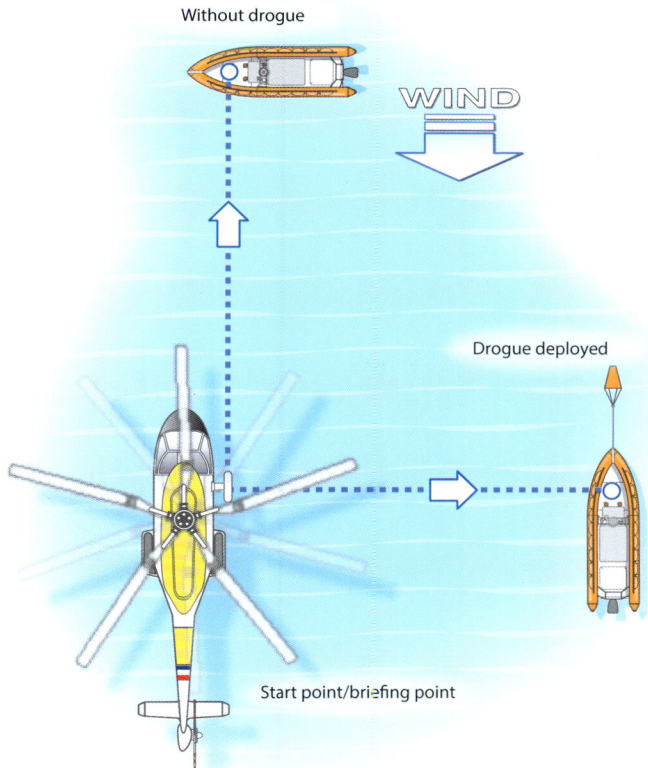

In the event of a static transfer, the vessel will typically lie beam-on to the wind. Deploying a sea anchor/drogue will stabilize the craft and reduce the likelihood of it being blown out of position due to the downdraught from the helicopter.

The helicopter will come into position and hover for one–two minutes to assess conditions and strategy before approaching.

13 RESCUE BY HELICOPTER

 ## Moving Transfers from Smaller Craft

These will only be undertaken by crews trained in these manoeuvres.

The helicopter will usually head directly into wind at 5–15 knots. The boat driver's role is to drive in steadily from the five o'clock position and hold directly under the winch.

Other boat crew will need to maintain forward lookout.

When the winch person is either on board or has departed, the vessel exits away to the two o'clock position.

An alternative method is based on the vessel 'ferry gliding' in from the 3 o'clock position then exiting to the 3 o'clock position once complete.

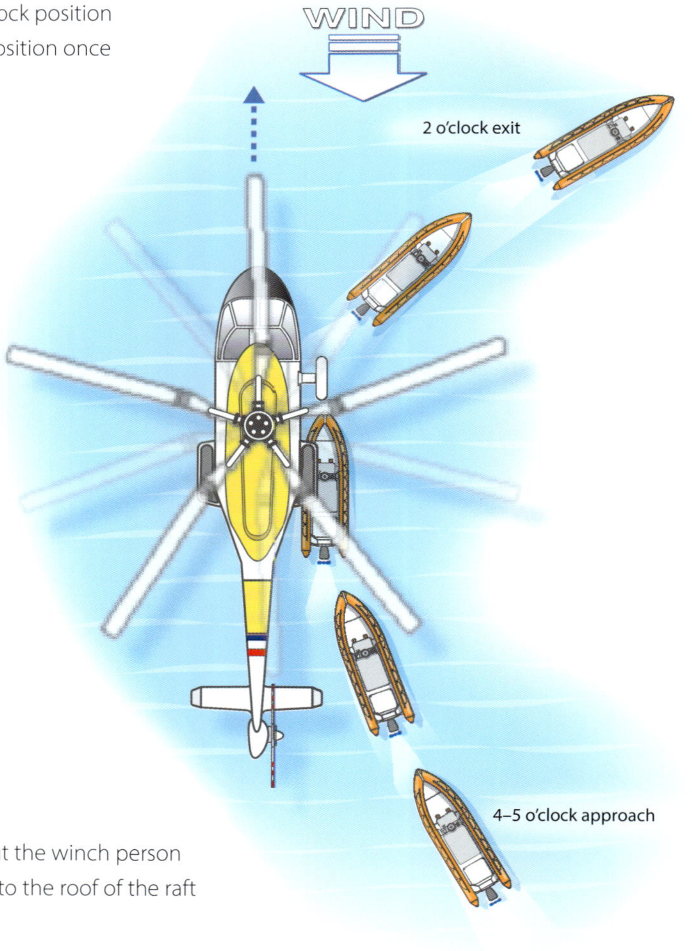

Lifting from a Liferaft

The principles are the same but the winch person may ask casualties to climb onto the roof of the raft and be extracted from there.

Chapter 14

Buoyancy and Stability

Understanding buoyancy and stability is essential to be able to helm a craft safely in any conditions. Changes to a vessel may affect stability and the safety of crew, passengers and vessel.

Buoyancy

A vessel in water displaces a volume of water, creating an upwards force. The point at which the force acts is known as the Centre of Buoyancy (CoB).

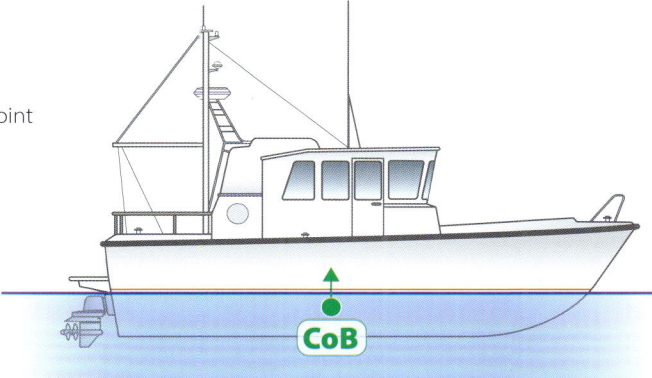

At rest, the position of the CoB is usually along the centre line of the vessel but, as the vessel moves due to wind or wave action, water in the bilges or movement of crew, the position of the CoB will vary.

The Centre of Gravity (CoG) is the point at which the mass of the vessel acts vertically downwards.

The point is fixed but moves with loading (people, fuel, water, waste, etc.) and as changes are made (e.g. a new liferaft fitted high rather than low in a craft). Bilge or deck water impacts too – see 'Free Surface Effect'.

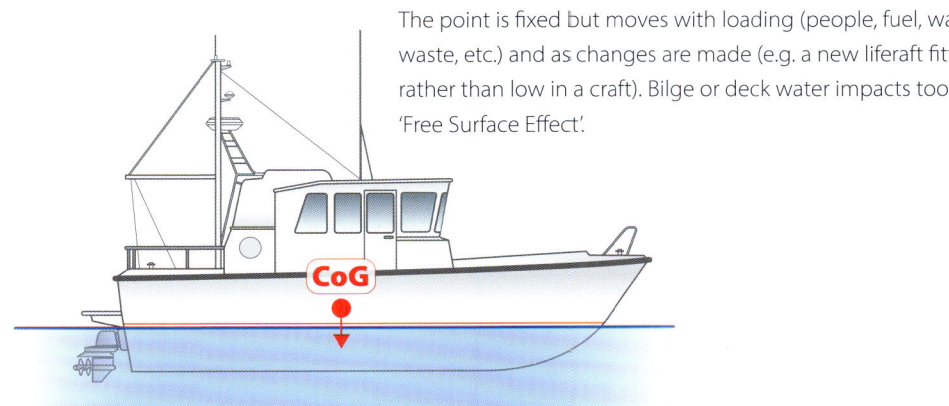

14 BUOYANCY AND STABILITY

Stability

A vessel is 'stable' if it returns to its original position when disturbed by external forces such as wind or waves.

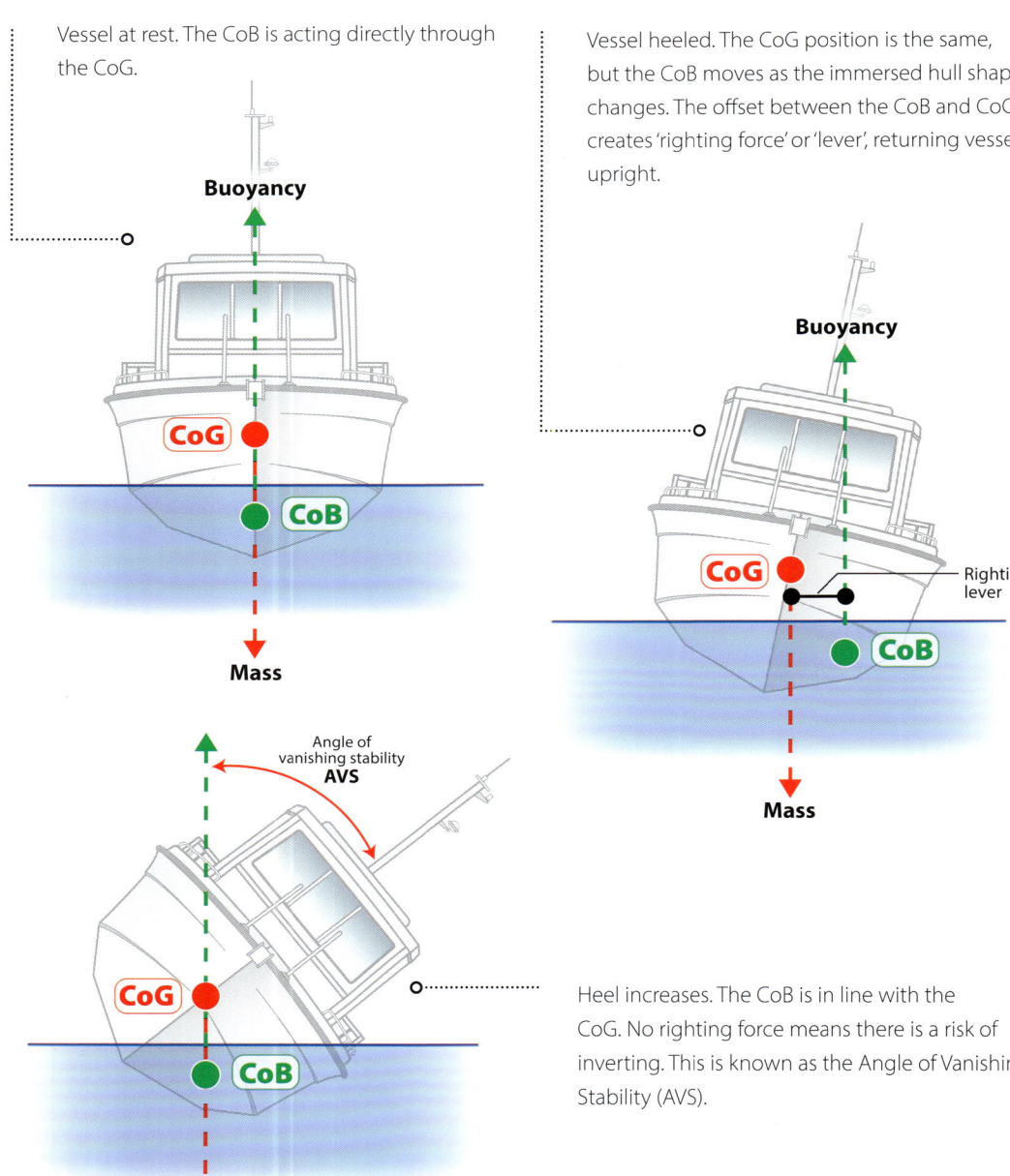

Vessel at rest. The CoB is acting directly through the CoG.

Vessel heeled. The CoG position is the same, but the CoB moves as the immersed hull shape changes. The offset between the CoB and CoG creates 'righting force' or 'lever', returning vessel upright.

Heel increases. The CoB is in line with the CoG. No righting force means there is a risk of inverting. This is known as the Angle of Vanishing Stability (AVS).

BUOYANCY AND STABILITY | 14

All vessels have a curve (the GZ (righting lever) Curve) linking the change of righting force with the angle of heel.

Designers increase the AVS by lowering the CoG and altering the position of the CoB. Some craft self-right – in these cases the position of the CoB generates a righting force, even though the vessel is inverted.

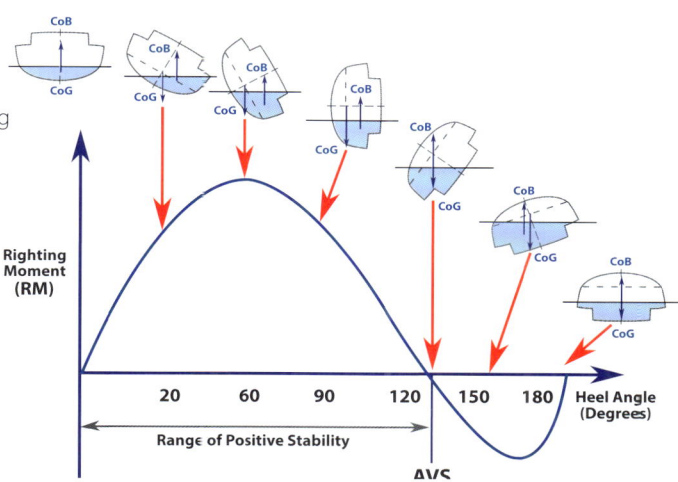

Free Surface Effect

Water in bilges or on deck that is unable to drain rapidly can have a devastating effect on stability.

The vessel has heeled but a righting force is present.

The vessel is heeled to the same angle, but water in the bilge moves the CoG to the point where the AVS is reached.

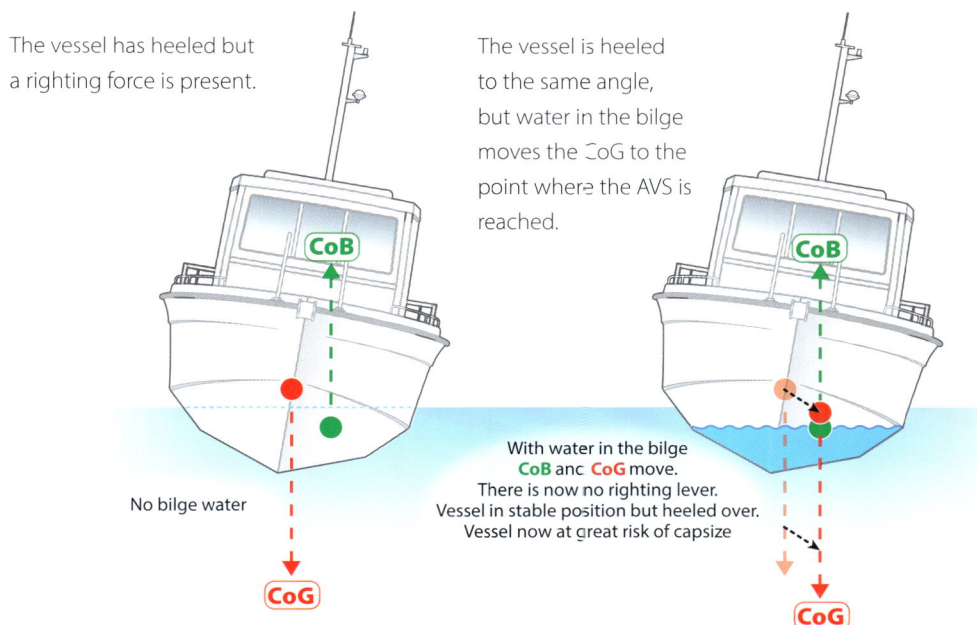

The ability to clear water rapidly from decks through scuppers, open transoms, and pumps is essential. Ensure bilge water is cleared and that pump capacity can cope with rapid water ingress. Beware low air intakes in rougher conditions.

Chapter 15

Wave Theory

Your ability to handle a craft in rougher conditions may be improved if you have an understanding of waves and some of the theory surrounding them.

Understanding a little about wave theory and the energy in waves may influence how you approach the waves you encounter when operating in rougher conditions.

Waves originate from two main sources:

Tide	Wind
Causes	
Horizontal water movement due to interaction of sun, earth and moon	Wind blowing across the surface of the sea
Factors affecting the size of waves	
Direction	Wind Speed
Rate	Duration
Obstructions	Fetch (The distance over the sea the wind has blown)

Wave Action/Terminology

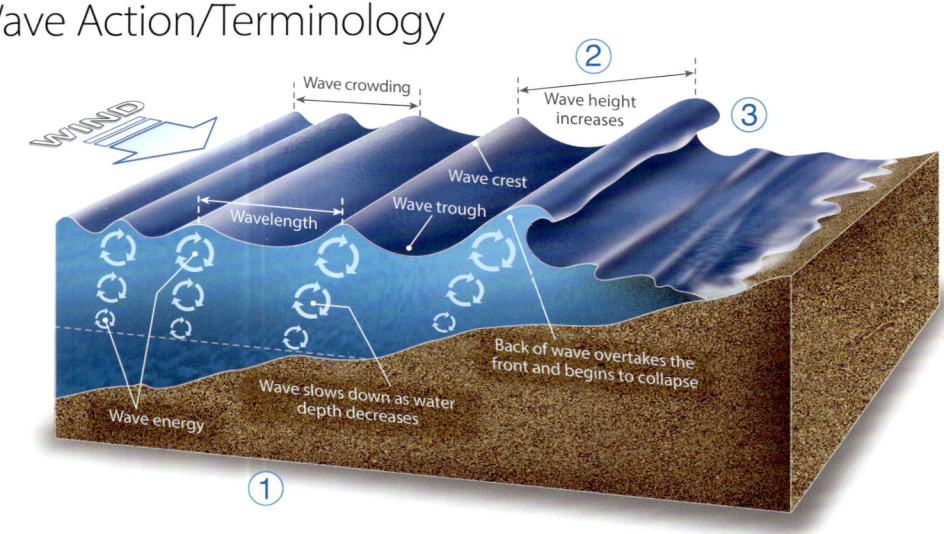

WAVE THEORY | 15

Lower wind gives shorter wavelength, slower waves and less energy.

Stronger wind gives longer wavelength, quicker waves and more energy.

The wave feels the bottom (1), energy is pushed up and the wave height increases (2). Waves become unstable and break (3).

Waves in shallow water tend to be choppier with shorter wavelengths, whereas those in deeper water tend to be smoother and rounder.

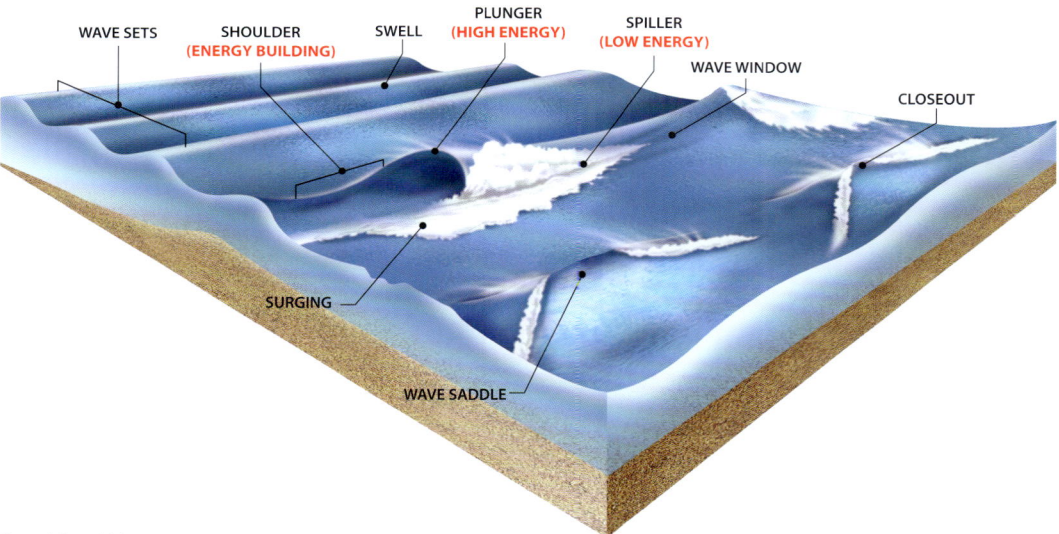

Breaking Waves

'Plungers': These have much greater energy than spillers so can be far more dangerous. The wave rises rapidly then collapses suddenly, releasing energy. Can occur at sea as well as close to shore as the seabed slope rapidly changes. More frequent in offshore winds.

'Spillers': Commonly seen as waves reach shore. Can occur in deeper water as the sea floor gradually shallows. The wave steepens and breaks, dissipating energy gradually in white water. More likely in onshore winds, they break for longer, and are usually relatively gentle.

Surging breakers: Usually occur on steep beaches. They are unlikely to have an impact unless beaching.

15 WAVE THEORY

Once the wind is reduced you get swell. Crests and troughs are smoother.

If the wind strength increases again, waves can form on top of the swell.

Wave direction may be the same or at any angle to the swell, depending on wind direction.

Tide-generated Waves

These arise from the horizontal movement of water over undulations in the seabed. With higher flow rates (spring tides), obstructions can create 'standing' (static) waves.

The flow rate also increases around headlands or through constrictions. Wind in the opposite direction may create severe conditions.

Wind Against Tidal (or Current) Stream

Wind in the same direction as the tide increases wavelength and flattens the sea. Wind opposed to tide shortens wavelength, increasing wave height.

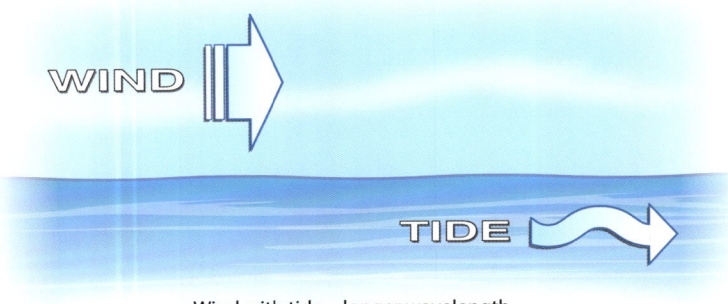

Wind with tide – longer wavelength

Wind against tide – shorter wavelength and steeper wave

WAVE THEORY | 15

Localised Conditions

Obstructions, islands and the shape of the seabed interact with waves to create localised conditions which may be dangerous. Considering wind direction, strength, rate and direction of stream when viewing a chart allows for prediction of these conditions. Chart symbols for eddies and overfalls will indicate potentially challenging conditions.

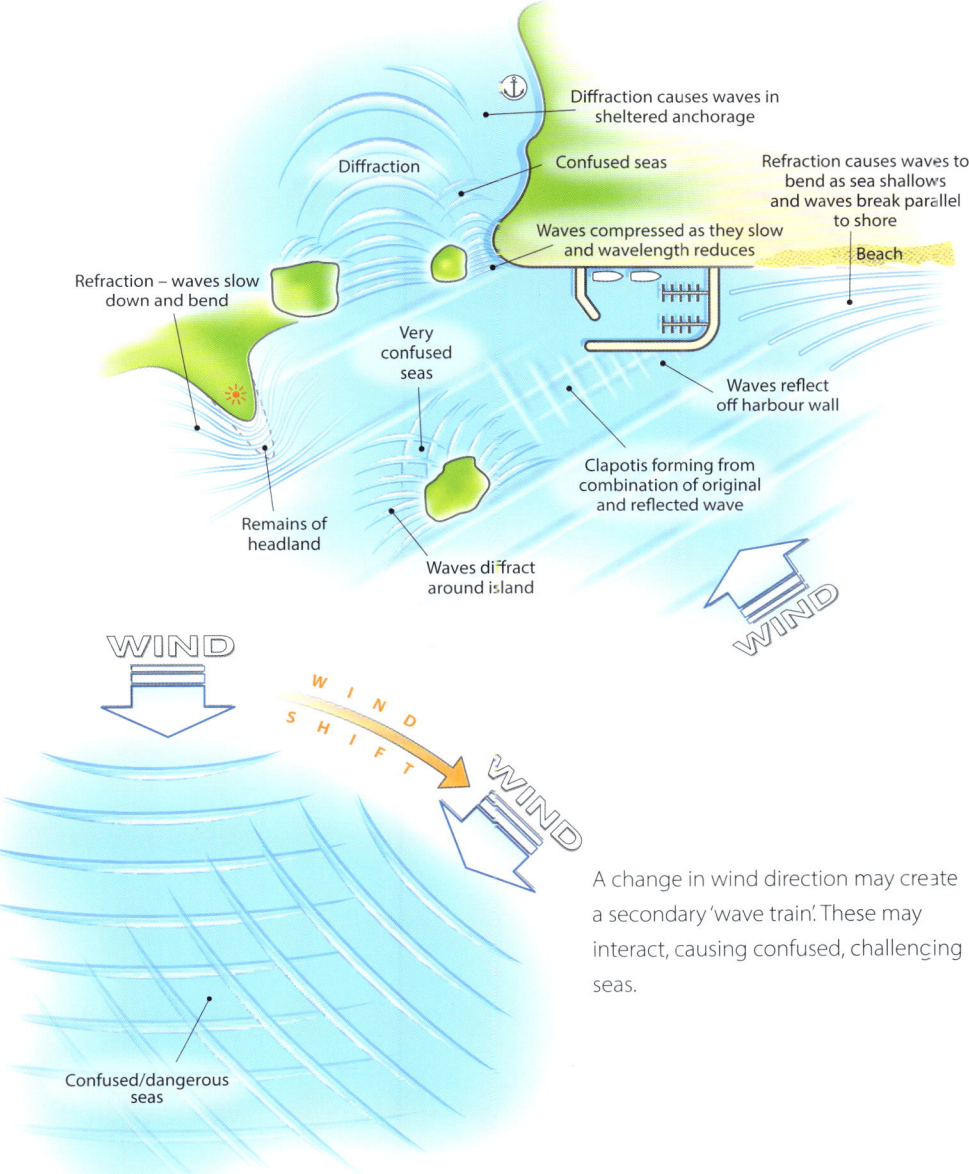

A change in wind direction may create a secondary 'wave train'. These may interact, causing confused, challenging seas.

15 WAVE THEORY

Sea State

The scale for sea state differs slightly to that for wind (the Beaufort Scale). To estimate wind strength and sea state, consider the fetch, depth, swell and tidal/current effects. Consider the time lag between the increase in wind and wave height.

Wind force	Wind speed	Description	Maximum likely wave height	Sea state – description	Sea state
0	< 1 knot	Calm	0m	Mirror-like	0
1	1–3 knots	Light air	Up to 0.1m	Ripples on the surface	1
2	4–6 knots	Light breeze	Up to 0.3m	Small wavelets with smooth crests	2
3	7–10 knots	Gentle breeze	Up to 0.9m	Large wavelets with crests starting to break	3
4	11–16 knots	Moderate breeze	Up to 1.5m	Large waves begin to form with white foam crests	3–4
5	17–21 knots	Fresh breeze	Up to 2.5m	Moderate waves and many white horses	4
6	22–27 knots	Strong breeze	Up to 4m	Large waves, spray and white foam crests	5
7	28–33 knots	Near gale	Up to 5.5m	Breaking waves, a heaped sea, lots of spray	5–6
8	34–40 knots	Gale	Up to 7.5m	Frequently breaking, moderately high waves	6–7
9	41–47 knots	Severe gale	Up to 10m	High waves, flying spray and breaking crests	7
10	48–55 knots	Storm	Up to 12.5m	Very high waves, almost totally white, with foam and spray	8
11	56–63 knots	Violent storm	Up to 16m	Extensive foam, exceptionally high waves, visibility seriously affected	8
12	> 64 knots	Hurricane	16m+	Air filled with foam and spray, very poor visibility	9

It is always possible that the sea state is less pronounced than wind strength; for example wind strength 6–7, sea state 3–4. This would be normal in areas such as harbours and estuaries where the fetch may be less, preventing the wind generating the wave state you would experience in open water.

Chapter 16

Handling in Rougher Water

Developing an ability to handle rougher conditions is an essential aspect of progressing as a powerboater. Nothing beats the hands-on experience of handling a craft in waves; however, care must be taken not to gain experience by placing you, your crew, vessel or rescue agencies in danger.

If faced with rougher conditions:

- Is your passage necessary? Knowing when to stay in port is the sign of a good skipper.
- Is there a safer alternative route?
- Is the craft suitable to face expected conditions? Are seating positions suitable to minimise fatigue and sustained wave impact?
- Are the crew fit enough, experienced, suitably clothed and understand the conditions?
- Is someone – coastguard, friends, employers – aware of the passage, its route and estimated timings?

16 HANDLING IN ROUGHER WATER

Preparation

- Secure loose items. Keep heavy items low.
- Hatches, portholes and unused seacocks should be closed.
- Bilges should be clear and pumps operating. Freeing ports should be clear and loose items that could block them should be stowed.
- Fuel filters should be clear – rougher conditions disturb sediment that could block filters. Have spares. Are fuel reserves sufficient for the passage?
- Lifesaving appliances should be ready, the grab bag prepared and easily to hand.
- Lifejackets and personal safety gear should be worn/available.
- A detailed safety brief should be delivered.

Rescue services should not need to come to your assistance for an unnecessary passage.

Types of Sea

Head sea (or 'up sea'): Heading into the wind/waves or on either bow.

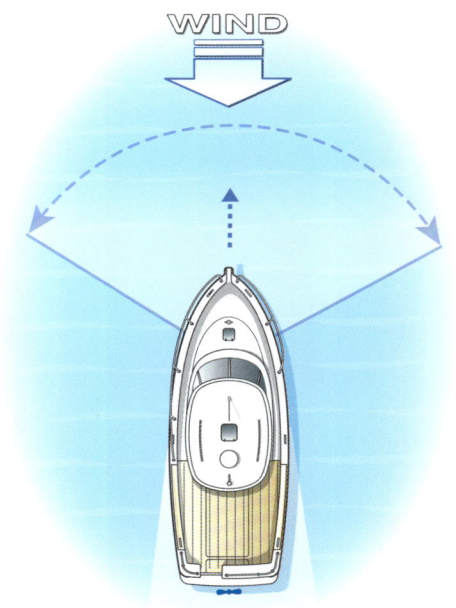

- The wave speed could be up to about 22 knots, so the combined boat/wave speed could be considerable, with severe impact forces on vessel and crew. Steep wave faces increase impacts, and waves get steeper as the wind increases.
- Trim the bow down to cut through waves. Too far 'down' (or 'in') may mean a very wet ride, as the bow may 'bury'. Adjust trim by 'feel' – each boat is different.
- Keeping your hands on the throttle and steering wheel allows instant reaction to oncoming waves.
- Work the throttle to adjust your 'angle of attack'.
- A longer wavelength gives more time to adjust the boat position.
- Very short wavelengths make it difficult to 'drive' – aim to limit impacts on the vessel and crew.

HANDLING IN ROUGHER WATER | 16

- Generally, you should throttle on through the trough and ease off towards the crest to keep the vessel in contact with the wave. When the bow drops over the crest then put the throttle on again. It may be necessary to increase power to punch through the top of the wave.

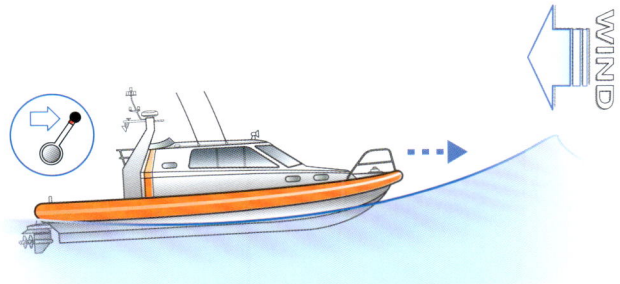

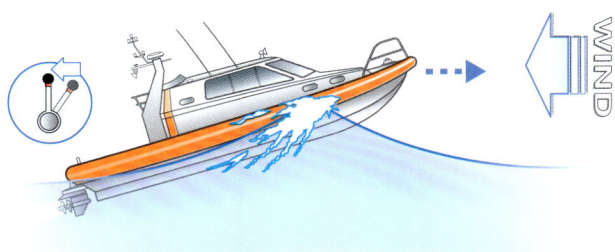

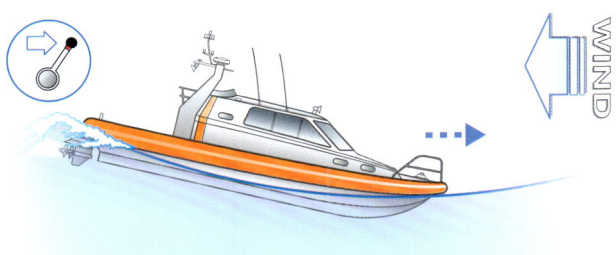

- Take larger, breaking waves head-on. Consider waiting and allowing the wave to break, and then power through the white water. The impact on the boat/crew is always greater as the wave breaks than just afterwards.

16 HANDLING IN ROUGHER WATER

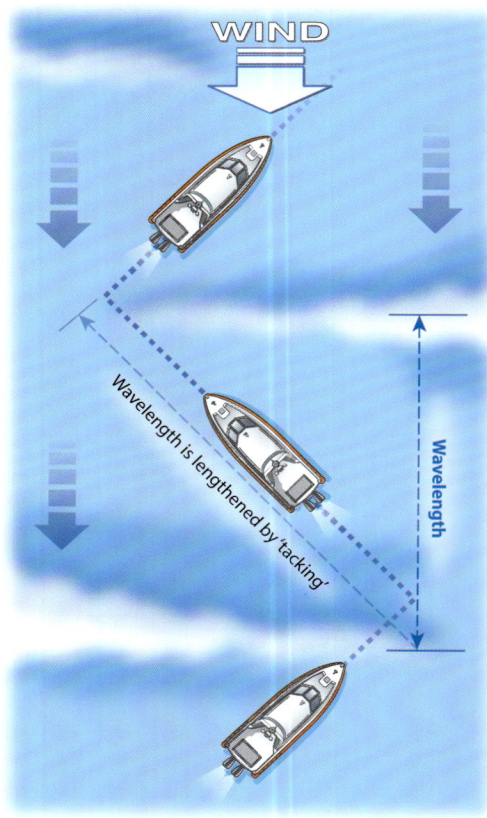

- A 'zig-zag' direction (tacking) upwind may be best – it increases wavelength and time between waves.
- Flying off waves may increase chances of injury, fatigue and damage, and may reduce speed of progress.
- For regular wave patterns find a speed at which the vessel contours waves, allowing steady progress without constant throttle adjustment. Maintain a sharp lookout for waves not matching the pattern.
- The buoyancy of the bow may aid handling by lessening the chances of the bow burying.
- You may be able to increase speed if the boat length in relation to wavelength allows the vessel to 'hop' from crest to crest. Considerable care is needed as there is a risk that the boat could plough into a wave face if the wavelength lengthens.

'Pendulum Effect'

A vessel heading upwind hits a wave at speed and clears the water. A light bow may be held by the wind, but a heavy stern continues forward, meaning a high chance of inversion.

The solution is simple: slow down!

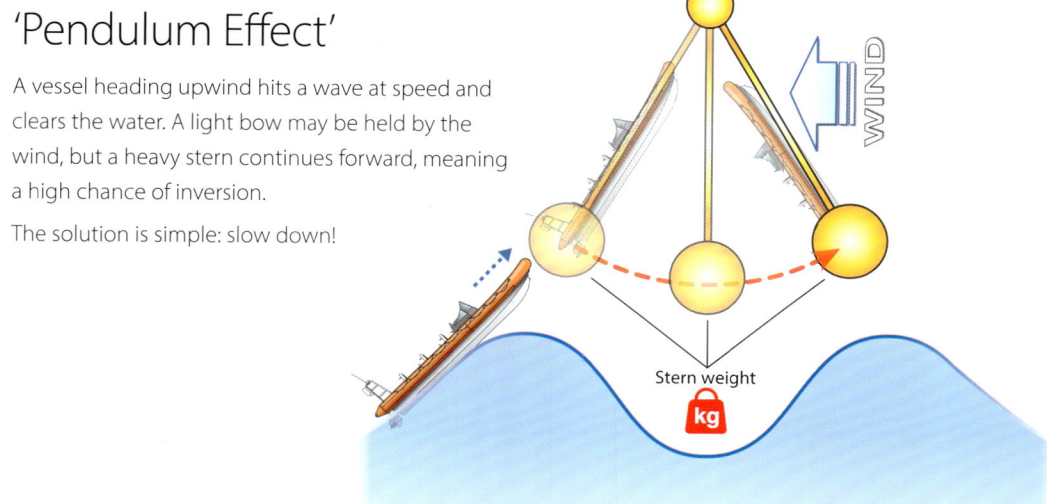

HANDLING IN ROUGHER WATER | 16

Following sea (or 'down sea'): Heading directly downwind or where it is taken on either quarter.

- The speed of encounter with waves is lower. The wind is behind the vessel so there is less spray and buffeting.
- However, risks can be greater due to complacency. A very real danger is driving the vessel over a wave and ploughing into the back of the next one, with the bow entering the wave. This is known as 'stuffing'. Rapid reduction of speed can cause considerable injury and damage, and the boat may fill with water, reducing manoeuvrability.
- Trim up (or out) to raise the bow and reduce the chances of stuffing. Optimum trim varies between craft.
- If the vessel 'stuffs', the following wave may pick up the stern, turn the vessel side on (broach) and roll the craft.

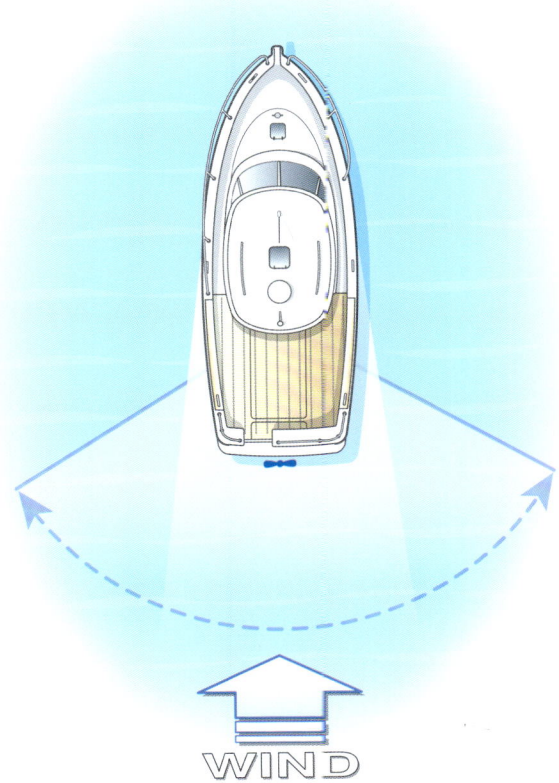

16 HANDLING IN ROUGHER WATER

- Good progress can be made by riding the back of the wave. Let it dissipate and power onto the back of the next wave.
- If possible, ride the largest wave as it gives the best 'height of eye'.

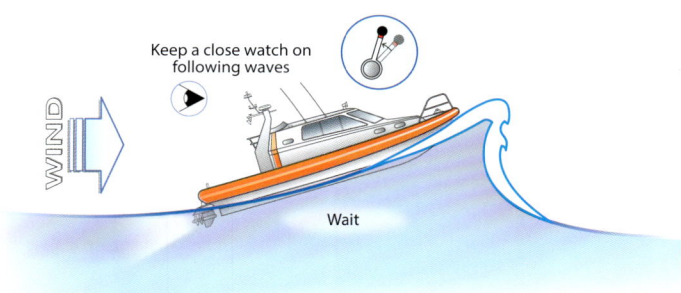

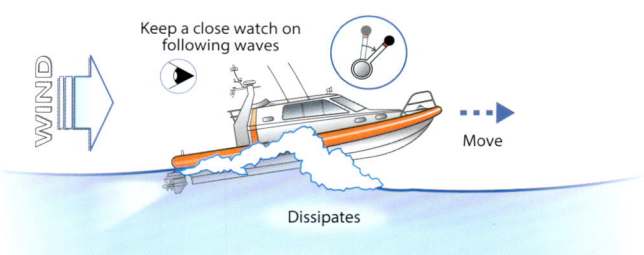

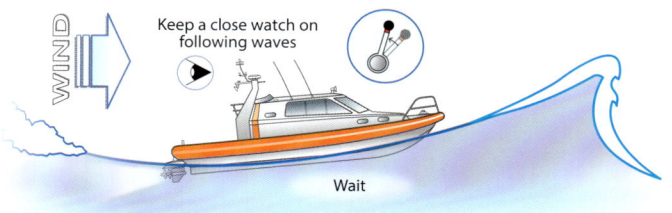

- Broaching can also occur if wave speed exceeds the vessel speed and lifts the stern, meaning the bow digs in and the vessel broaches. Manage vessel speed and position to stay clear of such waves. Perhaps tow heavy lines or stream a drogue to hold the stern.

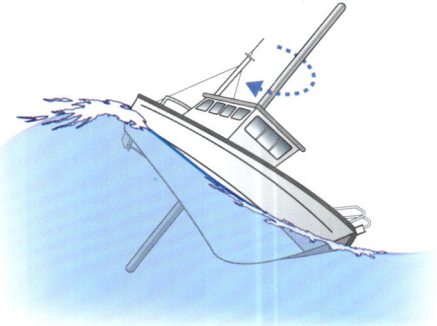
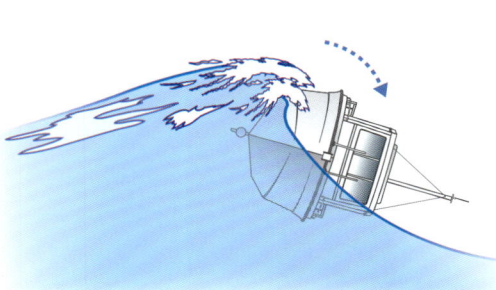

HANDLING IN ROUGHER WATER | 16

- Steering a path through waves is often possible.
- Keep a good lookout behind! Waves may catch the boat when you are running slower.
- Your speed through the water is far less and the effectiveness of rudders or outdrives is reduced, so handling ability is reduced too.
- Vessels with buoyant bows are less likely to stuff.

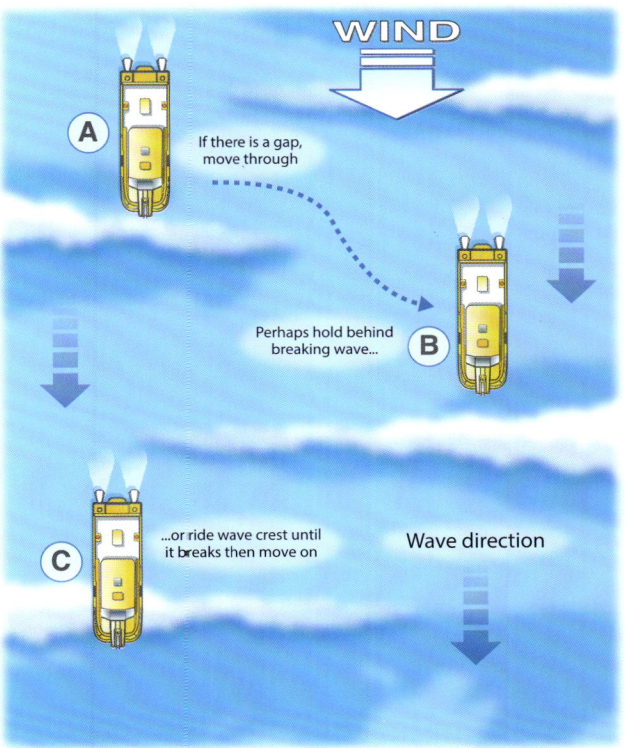

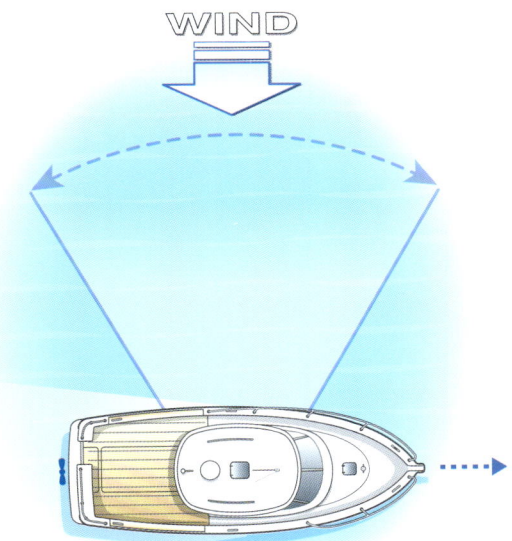

Beam sea: Heading roughly at right angles to the wind direction.

- Choose your route through troughs/crests to make good progress.
- The risk is usually from upwind. Beware breaking waves on beam and vary your speed/course to steer behind them.
- It is often possible to match your speed to conditions, enabling a fairly smooth ride.
- When downwind of a breaking wave, power away downwind and run down-sea to a position to turn, or if able turn and take the wave head on.

16 HANDLING IN ROUGHER WATER

- Ease the vessel over smaller breaking waves.
- Generally, a breaking wave of height equal or greater to the beam of the vessel will capsize it when taken on the beam.
- Always operate with reserves of power and speed.

Whatever the direction of travel, never relax. Always be prepared for wave impact.

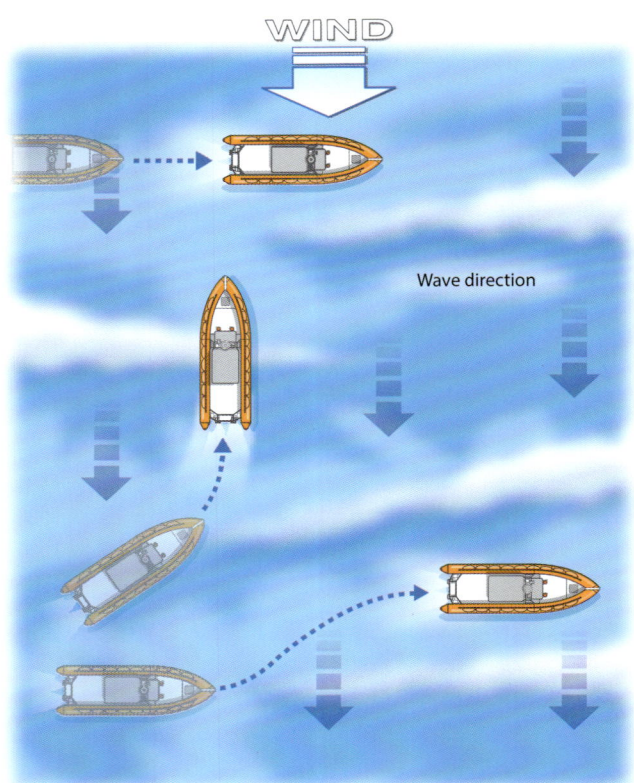

Dealing with Waves

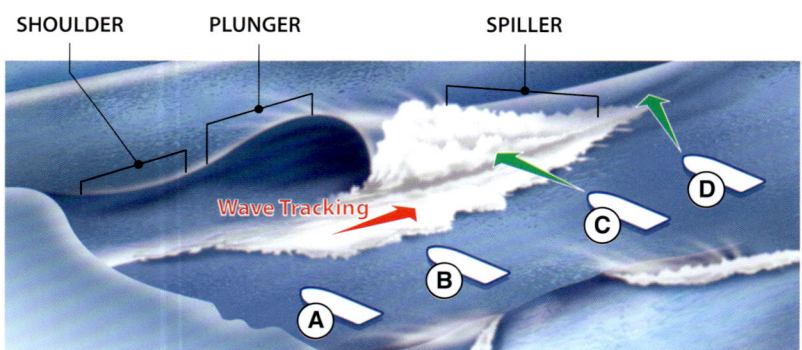

Vessel **A** is faced with the 'shoulder' of the wave. Energy is building and the wave may become a 'plunger', dissipating considerable energy as it breaks on the craft if it engages with the wave. Vessel **B** is faced with the plunger where the wave energy is at its greatest and would do well to hold back and let the wave break and energy dissipate. Vessel **C** is faced with a wave that has broken and the energy in the wave is rapidly dissipating. Proceeding ahead may be wet but the impact on the craft will be less. Vessel **D** is faced with a wave window and smooth progress.

HANDLING IN ROUGHER WATER | 16

Power On or Off?

If the stern clears the waves and the props are about to re-enter the water, the temptation is to reduce throttle. However, a short 'power on' of the throttle increases exhaust pressure and reduces the chances of water pushing up the exhaust and into the engine, which could disable it.

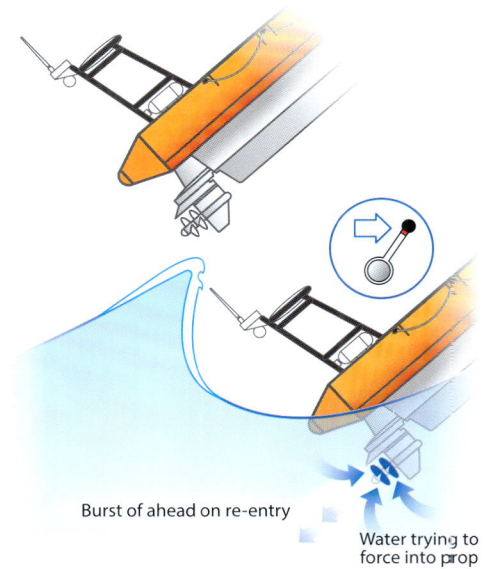

Burst of ahead on re-entry

Water trying to force into prop

Power v. Speed

The desire to make good progress has to be balanced with the safety of the vessel and crew. Excessive speed gives rise to the chance of injury, boat damage and the vessel being lost.

Use the craft's power to deal with rougher conditions. Avoid excessive speed. Always have reserves of power available – rarely should a craft be operated at full power.

Some organisations, though, may need to operate at high speeds in rougher conditions. Considerable care needs to be taken as the impacts the craft and crew will receive are significant. Apply the methods detailed but avoid high speed if possible and constantly monitor the effects on the vessel and crew.

Aerated Water and Ventilation

Aerated water is common in rougher conditions, creating 'ventilation'. Air drawn into the area of the propeller allows the engine to over-rev as the propeller struggles to bite. Steering may be less effective if the thrust or rudder is operating in aerated water. Jet-drive craft may suffer 'jet lag' in aerated water as it passes through the impeller.

Swell

Keep a good lookout as even large craft may be 'lost' in troughs. If the progress of another vessel synchronises with your own, they may not be visible until very close.

16 HANDLING IN ROUGHER WATER

Inlets and Bars

Shallower entrances to harbours or inlets can give rise to very rough conditions, especially if the wind is against the tide.

Consider delaying entrance or heading elsewhere until conditions improve. There tend to be small numbers of big waves. Once you are committed, a positive approach is needed. Concentrate totally and keep a good lookout behind in a following sea.

Know where the channel is on the other side of an area of rough water.

Resonant Rolling

Where a period of natural rolling motion is matched by a similar period in the waves, the rolling effect can materially increase. Change your course or speed to solve this.

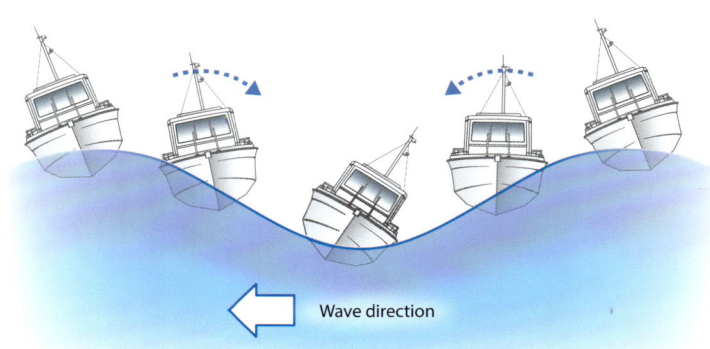

Wave direction

Craft Design

Understanding how your vessel handles in rougher conditions is essential. Shaft-drive vessels with rudders handle differently to outdrive-powered craft. Craft with significant buoyancy in the bow will react differently to a vessel with a thin bow and limited buoyancy. Some large diesel engines are turbocharged and suffer turbo lag before the power you need comes online, whilst other craft may have superchargers and turbochargers to overcome these issues.

Your approach to rougher conditions should be influenced by the vessel's configuration.

Sea Anchor

A key item of safety kit. It is deployed from the bow and enables the boat to hold head to wind rather than beam on. Rapidly deploying a sea anchor after engine failure may prevent a capsize.

Safety of Crew and Passengers

The number of repeated impacts on crew when transiting at even moderate speeds in rougher conditions can be considerable. Injury is common. Ensure the vessel is configured and driven appropriately for the conditions to limit the chance of injury.

Chapter 17

Higher-Speed Handling

Operating at higher speeds can be huge fun but driving faster places additional demands on the helm and requires specific skills. Those needing to drive fast for operational reasons are advised to undertake a fast-boat operators' course for that type of vessel.

The definition of 'fast' varies between vessels and may be 20 knots for some and 60 or 70 knots for others.

When driving at higher speeds the helm needs to be looking further ahead, interpreting wave conditions, looking for debris such as lobster pots etc. and identifying the risks posed by other craft. As with driving a motor vehicle the combined closing speeds of two craft can be considerable, so early decisions must be made. Crew should be deployed as additional lookouts and the helm should focus exclusively on the throttles/steering and not be distracted by any of the equipment on board.

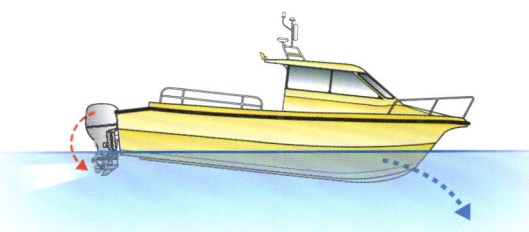

Trimming the bow up slightly (either by adjusting the sterndrives or using trim tabs) reduces the area of the hull in contact with the water ('the wetted surface'), increasing efficiency. Trim up too far and the vessel becomes unstable. Optimal trim position will vary according to conditions, loading etc. Experiment to determine the optimal position and ride.

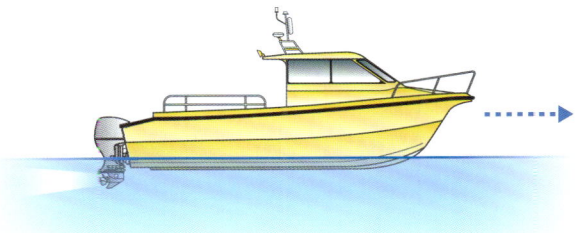

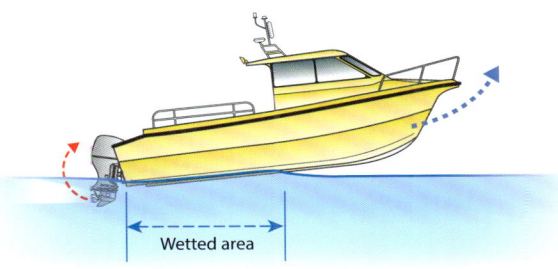

Wetted area

17 HIGHER-SPEED HANDLING

Unless too rough, it is usually possible to find and set a speed allowing the vessel to contour waves, creating a smoother ride. Too fast or slow and the vessel becomes out of sync, meaning the overall progress is slowed and the ride less comfortable.

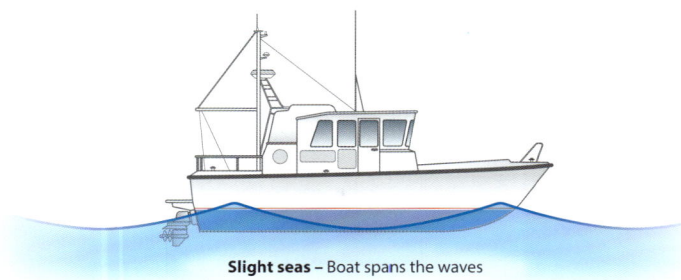

Slight seas – Boat spans the waves

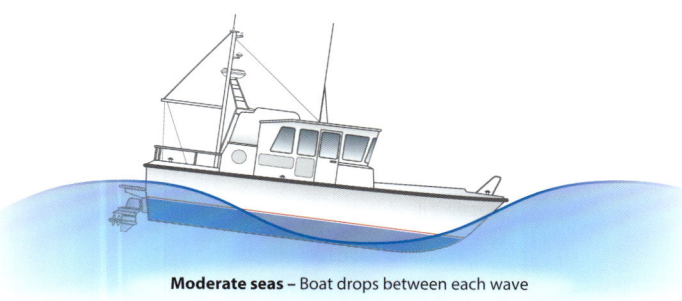

Moderate seas – Boat drops between each wave

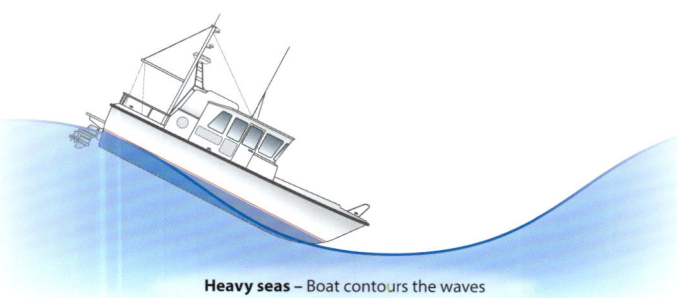

Heavy seas – Boat contours the waves

HIGHER-SPEED HANDLING | 17

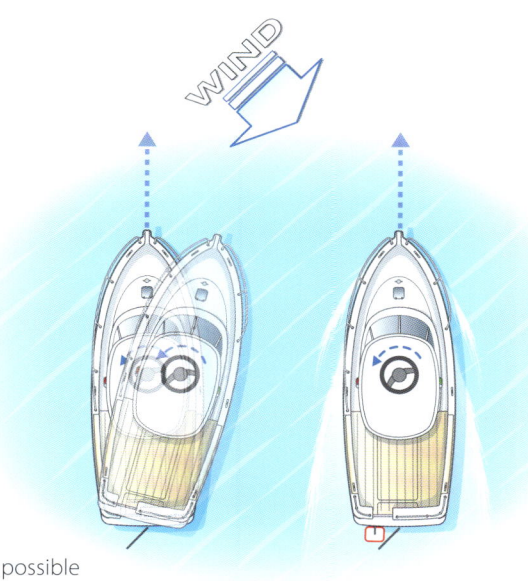

With the wind on the port or starboard bow it's possible that the vessel will heel into the wind as the driver applies steering to maintain heading.
Use trim tabs to level up.

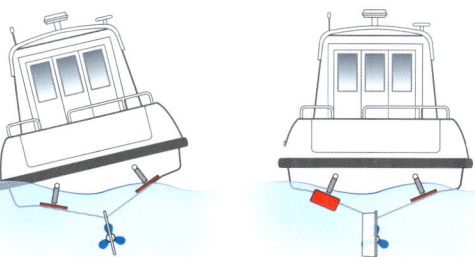

Depending on the wavelength, and the length of the vessel and its capability, it may be possible for the driver to increase speed and ride from crest to crest, creating a far smoother passage. Considerable care needs to be exercised, however, as the vessel may plough into an oncoming wave with considerable force if the wavelength suddenly increases.

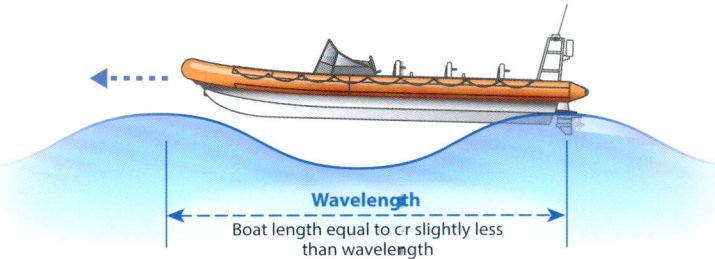

17 HIGHER-SPEED HANDLING

The helm should avoid rapid changes of direction at speed as crew and passengers may be subject to severe impacts and may be off-balance, considerably increasing the chances of injury.

As conditions get rougher it will be necessary to slow down. The safety of those on board and the vessel must take priority over the need to progress rapidly.

The helm must always keep one hand on or alongside the throttles so that they can react to conditions or changes to wave patterns. Steering/engine failure at higher speeds can be catastrophic – reducing power immediately is critical.

A good lookout is essential. Detail a crew member to assist with looking for other vessels or objects in the water. In calm conditions, wash from other vessels may be a risk if not spotted early.

High-speed operations may expose crew to considerable repetitive impacts. Operators must work to understand and limit the exposure of those on board. The craft should be set up to lessen the impacts on crew for higher-speed operations.

GNSS 'Lag'

At higher speeds the position shown for the vessel on the GNSS/chartplotter system may be behind the real position as a result of the delay in calculating the vessel's position due to its speed.

This may create a serious danger if the GNSS/chartplotter is used to navigate at speed between two areas of danger. The plotter may show the craft nearer to one island, leading the helm to compensate, but the time delay in the GNSS means that the helm has compensated for an error that actually didn't exist, placing the craft nearer the rock on the other side of the channel.

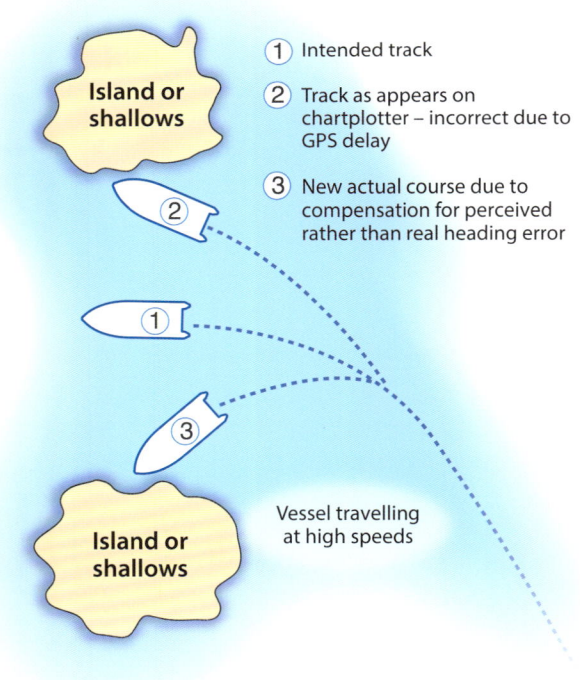

Chapter 18

Transfers between Moving Craft

There is sometimes a need to helm a vessel to bring it alongside another moving craft in order to transfer equipment, personnel or perhaps a boarding team.

Bringing two craft alongside each other when moving has considerable potential for injury to people and damage to craft, and should only ever be performed by experienced helm. Those needing to perform these manoeuvres should undertake specific training.

When a vessel is under way there are pressure zones around it. Positive zones tend to push craft apart; negative zones may draw vessels together.

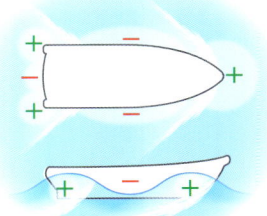

Determine your approach – generally, use the protected leeward side. Communicate before the approach to agree the speed (typically the minimum speed at which steerage can be maintained, which is usually about 6–10 knots) for the target vessel and the course, abort signals, transfer commands and communication channel for helms who may not be in sight. Identify the transfer location where you will place your vessel – this will usually be towards the centre of the vessel or aft of this point.

Assign responsibility for forward lookout and communications to a crew member as the helm will be totally focused on the target vessel.

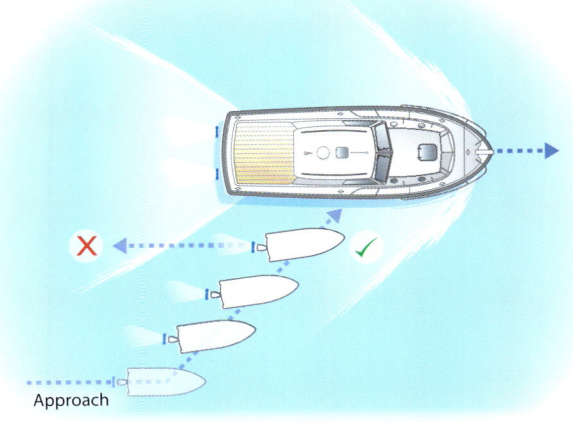
Approach

Don't drop back through the stern wake as it may act like a breaking wave. Ferry glide in steadily, keeping roughly parallel. Equally, don't push too far forward under the bow of the target craft.

18 TRANSFERS BETWEEN MOVING CRAFT

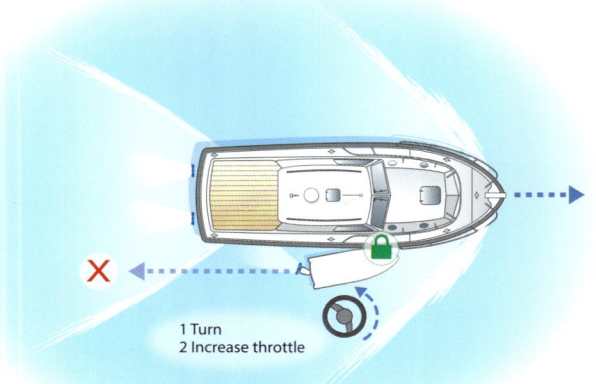

1 Turn
2 Increase throttle

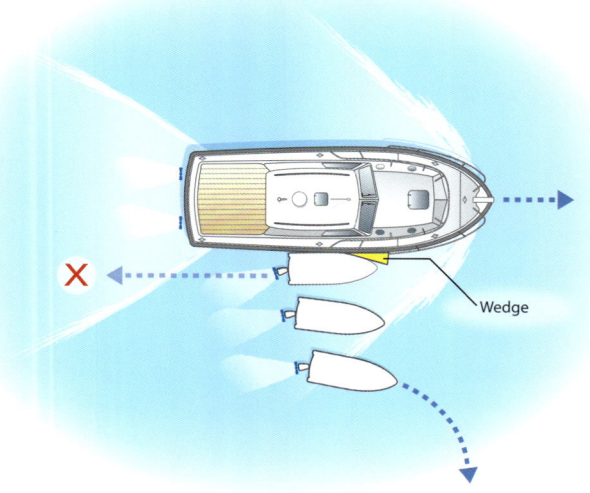

Wedge

Chapter 19

Towing

Being able to come to the assistance of a fellow boater and offer a tow is an essential skill. Knowing when to insist on professional assistance is the sign of a good skipper.

Detailed information about undertaking long tows (or 'in-line' tows) and alongside tows is covered in the RYA Powerboat Handbook (G13), so is not repeated here in full.

Skippers operating at an advanced level are far more likely to become actively involved in undertaking or requiring a tow, so they should ensure that they are familiar with and practise the relevant techniques.

Long tow: For open water when towing a disabled craft behind.

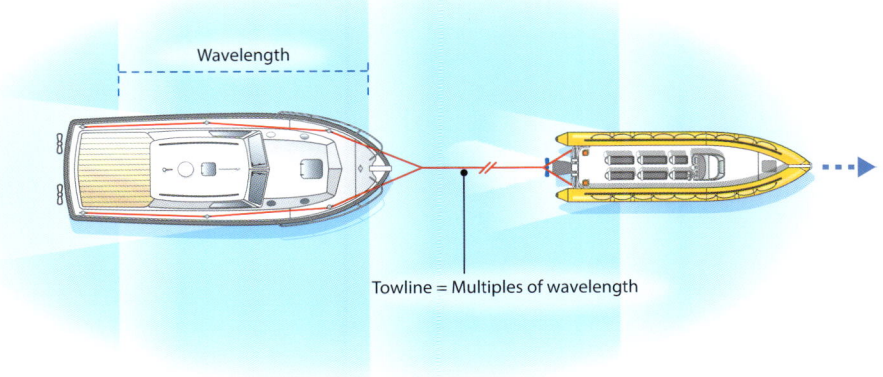

Key points:
- Ensure the towline is as long as possible, especially in rougher conditions.
- Match the towline length to wavelength if possible.
- Weighting the towline will reduce snatch loading.
- Spread the load between the cleats of the towed vessel unless towing from a D-ring.

RYA ADVANCED POWERBOAT HANDBOOK 131

19 TOWING

Alongside or 'side' tow: For harbours or marinas, when requiring precision manoeuvring.

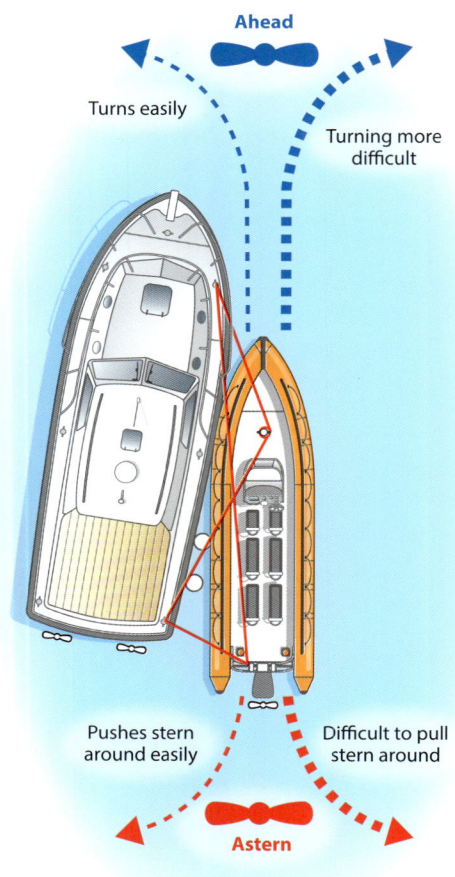

- Boat positioning and rigging of spring lines is key.
- Treat the vessel as a very wide twin-engine craft. In this example turns to port will be easy but starboard may be very difficult until the vessel has some momentum.
- Vessels should be well fendered.

Tips for Towing

With a long tow it can be difficult to vary the towline length if it is secured to a bridle at the stern of the towing vessel.

TOWING | 19

Being able to vary the towline length is beneficial, especially when entering a harbour where the towline length will generally need to be far shorter than in open water and rougher conditions.

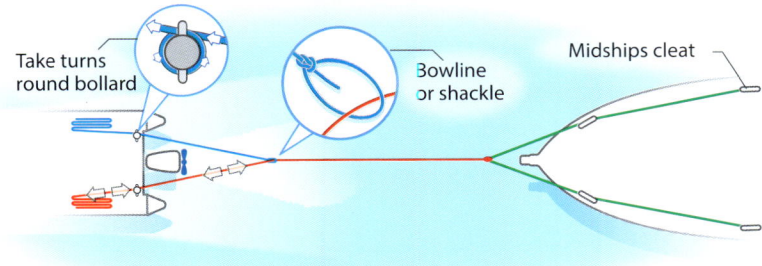

This method allows the length of the towline to be varied easily from within the towing craft.

A method that may also be useful in certain situations is bow-to-bow towing. This is only suitable for fairly calm conditions and allows the towing craft rapidly to get a single line on and establish control of the disabled craft. It can work well where the disabled craft is in shallow water or against an obstruction and there is a need to keep the towing vessel's prop(s) in deeper or clearer water. Typically this tow will just be used to pull the vessel into clear water, where a long or alongside tow can be rigged.

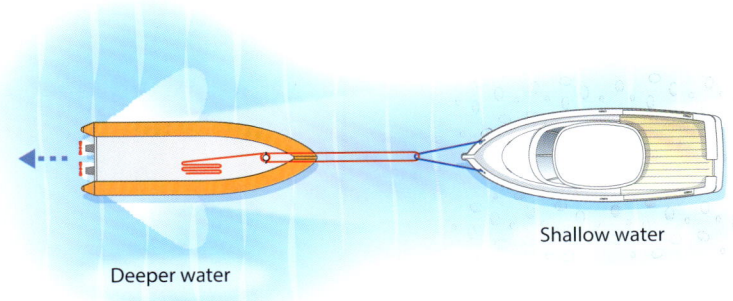

If possible, rig a line through a D-ring or around a cleat on the disabled craft, allowing the towing craft to vary the tow length easily or release rapidly. Fittings on both craft must be suitable for the tow.

Whether you are the towing or towed vessel, always ask:

- Is the craft suitable to undertake a tow? Are there suitable strong points to tow from? What power is required versus the weight of craft and how long or strong does the line need to be?
- Do the crew and helm have appropriate experience? It may be better to stand by and wait for the rescue services or a commercial tow.
- Is it safe to set up and undertake the tow?

Always alert the rescue services early to an incident.

RYA ADVANCED POWERBOAT HANDBOOK

Chapter 20

Cruising

Exploring new areas can be great fun but taking your boat further afield raises new challenges. There is a need to plan carefully and ensure that your vessel is suitable and properly equipped for the passage you intend to undertake.

A small boat cruise can range from a few miles to many hundreds or even thousands of miles. The best way to start is to cruise in company with experienced skippers and crews, where you can learn from others who have done it before. The chance to watch them, understand how they have prepared and planned and even look at how they have set up their boats can be invaluable. Joining a club or an event run by a marina is a great way to get involved.

The type of boat you have will influence to a large degree where you can go and what conditions are sensible to go out in. Long-distance cruising in smaller boats tends to be the domain of RIBs but, in the right conditions, smaller sportsboats can cover significant distances.

CRUISING 20

A boat prepared for longer cruising will need to carry a full supply of spares, an expanded toolkit, an enhanced medical kit, more than one chartplotter/GNSS, and additional means of issuing distress, almost certainly including an EPIRB. It will either be a twin-engine craft, always run with another vessel, or have an auxiliary engine. The demands and stresses placed on the boat will differ over longer distances and it is essential that kit is stowed properly or tied down, and that engines and electronics are working perfectly.

In smaller, open craft it is essential that crew are adequately clothed. This may mean a drysuit or immersion suit. A helmet and goggles will significantly increase comfort and safety in less favourable conditions. A hand-held VHF attached to the lifejacket, a personal locator beacon and a personal flare are strongly advised, allowing the crew member to issue distress from the water if they get thrown overboard.

In addition to having the right kit and preparing the boat properly, the skipper's experience and knowledge needs to be greater too, as they will need to be far more self-sufficient. Consider undertaking tailored training, including engine courses specific to your own vessel.

Planning fuel usage and where you can refuel is key. In many areas petrol is not available shoreside and filling plastic cans from petrol stations is increasingly difficult. In some areas even diesel is not available, but a harbourmaster will usually be able to arrange a delivery. Carrying a large funnel is essential. Any plan should always ensure that the fuel level never drops below one-third full.

Good planning dictates that a skipper should have pilotage plans prepared for all ports of entry, including possible ports of refuge.

One of the challenges facing the skipper will be assessing weather information and deciding whether to undertake the passage or stay in port. Many factors will influence the decision, including the capability of the vessel, the crew, how exposed the cruising area is and the ease of seeking refuge in the event that the weather is worse than predicted. Where to get the required weather information will depend where you are cruising – if you are new to an area, seeking advice from local commercial boaters is often a good idea.

Cruising can take the form of an endurance event, where the aim may be to cover large distances during the day, or may focus on exploring a rugged coastline in great detail. Any mixture of the two is fine but ensure that, as skipper, you choose a cruise that suits all of your crew. Too often a wonderful coastline is seen from afar as the need to get from A to B reduces the time to see and experience wonderful sights on route.

Glossary

AIS	Automatic Identification System
Almanac	Publication containing information about ports and harbours including tidal heights/curves. Published annually
Anticyclone	High-pressure weather system
AVS	Angle of Vanishing Stability – angle from the vertical beyond which a craft will no longer return upright but will capsize
Back bearing	A bearing taken astern of a craft (using a hand bearing compass) to a feature to ensure vessel stays on intended track
Bearing	Direction of one object from another
Beaufort scale	International scale of wind speed and wave height
Broaching	When a vessel becomes broadside to a wave and is rolled onto its side
'Bucket'	Alternative term for the deflector used on jet drives to redirect water flow
Chart datum	The vertical level to which charts are drawn representing the Lowest Astronomical Tide ('LAT')
Chartplotter	Electronic charting system using the GNSS system. May use scanned ('raster') or digital ('vector') charts
Clearing lines/ranges	Position lines/ranges to clear hazards on charts/chartplotters
'ColRegs'	Collision regulations (International Regulations for Preventing Collisions at Sea – IRPCS)
Commercial endorsement	Qualification required to be able to work at sea
Compass rose	Representations of compass card on chart
Contour lines	Lines on charts linking points of equal depth
Course Over Ground ('COG')	The course a craft is proceeding along although the craft may not be pointing in this direction
'Crabbing'	Moving sideways without any ahead/astern movement
Cross bearing	Bearing on object to port or starboard of vessel
Day shapes	Spheres or cones (or combinations of) raised during daytime to indicate reason why vessel's movement may be constrained
Dead reckoning	Position based on time, distance and direction travelled through water from known position
Deflector	Used on jet drives to redirect water flow
Depression	Low-pressure weather system
Deviation	Compass error caused by presence of electromagnetic fields or ferrous objects
Displacement hull	Traditional hull shape where craft moves through (displaces) the water
DSC	Digital Selective Calling system, part of a VHF radio
EBL	Electronic bearing line. Found on radar to measure bearings to an object
EPIRB	Emergency Position Indicating Radio Beacon
Ergonomics	Study of efficiency of persons in working environment such as how instruments and controls are laid out for a helm
Estimated position	Dead reckoning but with tidal stream added in too
Ferry gliding	Technique for moving a craft sideways balancing stream or wind, the angle of the craft and ahead/astern throttle
Forward-facing drive	Pivoting drive system through hull of craft with propellers facing forwards

Glossary

Free surface effect	Loss of stability of vessel resulting from water in bilges or on deck that is unable to drain rapidly
GNSS	Global Navigation Satellite System
Ground track	Direction the craft is actually moving over surface of the earth
Head bearing	A bearing taken ahead of a craft (using a hand bearing compass) to a feature to ensure vessel stays on intended track
Heading	Direction in which vessel is actually pointing at any given moment
Helm	Steering; person who is steering (also helmsman/helmswoman)
Horizontal chart datum	The datum the chart is drawn to – e.g. WGS84
IMO	International Maritime Organisation
Impeller	The term given to the propeller encased in a jet-drive unit
IRPCS	International Regulations for Preventing Collisions at Sea ('ColRegs')
Jet drive	Drive system where water is pumped through a steerable nozzle to create thrust and turn a craft
'Jockey' seats	Seats found in RIBs where occupant sits astride the seat
Joystick system	Control system using multi-directional lever both to steer and adjust throttle(s)
Latitude	Lines bisecting the earth horizontally expressed as an angle relative to the equator and measured in degrees and minutes
Leeway	Effect of wind on vessel pushing it away from intended track
Longitude	Lines drawn between the poles referred to as east or west of the prime meridian (the 'zero' line through Greenwich) and measured in degrees and minutes
MARPA	Mini Automatic Radar Plotting Aid
MARPOL	International Convention for the Prevention of Pollution from Ships
MMSI	Maritime Mobile Service Identity, the unique number allocated by a country's licensing authority for VHF radios fitted with DSC
MOB	Man Overboard
MRCCs	Maritime Rescue Co-ordination Centres
Mullions	Vertical bars between the windows in a vessel's cabin
NDP	Nominated Departure Point for vessel's operating licence
Neap tides	Where the sun and moon act at right angles to the earth leading to more moderate high and low tides
Outdrive	Drive system through stern combining benefits of inboard and outboard engines, not requiring separate rudder
'Paddlewheel effect'	see 'Propwalk'
Pilotage	Navigation of vessel within close proximity to land, visible objects etc.
Pivot points	Point in the craft about which it pivots – varies between astern and forward
Planing hull	Hull shape which, on gaining speed, enables the craft to travel on the surface of water
'Propwalk'	Sideways movement of stern caused by rotation of propeller in reverse
Raster chart	Direct electronic copy or scan of existing paper chart
RIB	Rigid Inflatable Boat constructed with inflatable sponsons ('tubes') attached to a rigid hull. Also referred to as a RHIB – Rigid Hull Inflatable Boat

Glossary

Rule of Twelfths	Mathematical process for estimating height of tide at given time between High and Low Water
Safe haven	A place that a vessel could seek shelter in poor conditions. A term relevant to the licensing of commercial craft
Secondary ports	Smaller ports which don't have their own tidal curve in an almanac. An adjustment process is used to utilise a tidal curve from a standard port
Semi-displacement hull	Hull shape combining the benefits of displacement and planing types
Shaftdrives	Drive system for inboard engines utilising a shaft rotating the propeller and a rudder for steerage
SOLAS	International Convention for the Safety of Life at Sea. SOLAS V indicates Chapter 5
Speed Over Ground ('SOG')	The actual speed a craft is achieving after stream and wind have been factored in
Spring tides	Where the sun and moon act together to produce higher high tides and lower low tides
Springs	Mooring lines run diagonally from boat to berth to arrest/limit forward/astern movement of the craft
Standard ports	Larger ports that appear in almanacs with their own tidal curve and tidal data
STCW	International Convention on Standards of Training, Certification and Watchkeeping for Seafarers
Stream	Movement of water caused by tide or river flow
Strum box	Strainer on the bilge end of the bilge-pump pipe
'Stuffing'	Where, typically, in a following sea, a craft is driven over a wave and ploughs into back of the next one
Synoptic charts	Weather charts giving a general view of weather conditions
Thruster – bow or stern	Small sideways-mounted electrically powered prop in bow (and sometimes the stern) to aid close-quarter control
Tidal streams	Horizontal movements of tides
Tidal vector	Line drawn on chart representing direction and flow of tide
Transit	Lining up two fixed objects either to navigate along or to establish position with
Trim	Changing the boat's attitude for best safety, comfort, fuel consumption and handling
Trim tabs	Electrically or mechanically driven plates mounted either side of stern to adjust trim
TSS	Traffic Separation Scheme
UNCLOS	United Nations Convention on the Law of the Sea
Variation	Difference between Magnetic North and True North
Vector chart	Digitised version of a paper chart with ability to select/hide some information
VRM	Variable Range Marker. Found on radar, often used to measure distance to an object
Waypoints	GNSS position-storing facility
WGS84	World Geodetic System 1984 datum standard
Williamson Turn	Method of turning to return along vessel's own wake
Windage	Wind resistance of side area of boat
XTE	'Cross-track error', also known as 'off course' distance to one side of the exact track between two waypoints

Index

A

AIS (Automatic Identification System)	78, 81
personal	93
SARTs (Search and Rescue Transponders)	94
almanacs	72, 74
Angle of Vanishing Stability (AVS)	108, 109

B

Beaufort wind scale	85
belts, engine	19
bilge pumps	89, 109, 116
boat, choice of	10–14
boat, types of	see craft, types of
boat equipment	94, 135
boat handling	21–35
bow into wind, keeping	23
control, maintaining	23
factors affecting	21–23
'ferry gliding'	22, 129
forward-facing drives	29
higher-speed	see higher-speed boat handling
jet drives	see jet drives, boat handling with
leverage with twin outdrives/outboards	23
manoeuvring in marinas	see manoeuvring in marinas
momentum	23
outdrive- or outboard-powered craft	24–25
single engine	24
twin engines	23, 24–25
pivot points	22, 30
'propwalk'	22, 25
in rougher water	see rougher water, boat handling in
shaftdrives	25–26
and stream	22
thrusters	25, 29
trim tabs	35
and wind	21, 23
bow thrusters	25, 29
breezes, land and sea	86–87
buoyage light characteristics	54
and position fixing	59
buoyancy	107, 108

C

care of craft	19–20 see also emergency situations
catamarans	11
Centre of Buoyancy (CoB)	107, 108, 109
Centre of Gravity (CoG)	107, 108, 109
chart datums, horizontal	68
chartplotters	50–51, 64–65 see also waypoint(s) entries
choosing	65
'Course to Steer', calculating	61–62
over more than one hour	62
'Cross Track Error' (XTE)	55, 58
Estimated Position (EP)	60, 62
'lag'	128
layout	64
Man Overboard Button	64, 89, 90
options	64
and position fixing	57
searching and search patterns	97, 101
'Speed Over Ground' (SOG)	51, 64
and tides	72, 76
charts	68–71
electronic	50, 58, 69
techniques	69–71
bearing and range	69
distance, measuring	70
position, plotting	70–71
range and bearing	69
types compared	68
chartwork symbols	63
checks, daily	15, 19, 94 see also emergency situations
collision avoidance and radar	80
collision regulations ('ColRegs')	8, 9, 36–47
crossing situations	39
head-on situations	38
keeping clear	37
key rules	36
lights	43–46
narrow channels	41
overtaking	40
risk of collision, assessing	37
sailing craft	40–41, 43
shapes, day	43, 44–45, 46
sound signals	42, 47, 85
Traffic Separation Schemes (TSS)	41
visibility, restricted	42, 47, 85
commercial craft licensing requirements	17–18
commercial endorsement	8, 9
communication with crew	6

Index

compass	65
and deviation	71
compass rose waypoint	58
control systems	14
craft, choice of	10–14
craft, moving, transfers between	129–130
craft, types of	10–14
catamarans	11
displacement hull	11
planing hull	11
RIBs	15, 16, 89
semi-displacement hull	11
craft design	124
craft layout	15
crew, communication with	6
crew protection	7, 15–16, 124, 128
cruising	134–135
equipment	135
fuel usage	135
planning	135
weather conditions	135
current, wind against	112–113
current and boat handling	22

D

deviation	71
distance v. speed v. time	66
distress, responding to	9, 95
drive systems	13 *see also* forward-facing drives; jet drives; outdrives; shaftdrives

E

emergency situations	88–89 *see also* helicopter rescue; searching and search patterns
fire	89
fuel	89
hull, porthole or tube damage	89
man overboard *see* man overboard	
overheating	89
water ingress	88
engine control systems	14, 29
engines	12
access to	15
daily checks	15
overheating	89
EPIRBs (Emergency Position Indicating Radio Beacons)	93, 94, 135
equipment, boat and personal	93, 94, 135

F

fault-finding and fixing	19–20 *see also* emergency situations
'ferry gliding'	22, 129
fire	89
flares, personal	93, 135
fog	42, 47, 85
footstraps	16
forward-facing drives	13, 29
fuel	89, 135
fuel filters	19, 89, 116

G

GNSS (Global Navigation Satellite System)	50, 57, 64, 65 *see also* chartplotters
'lag'	128
Man Overboard Button	64, 89, 90
searching and search patterns	97, 101
grab bag	116

H

helicopter rescue	102–106
heaving-in line ('Hi-Line') transfer	104–105
lifting from liferaft	106
moving transfers from smaller craft	106
preparation	103
vertical transfer	103
helm/navigator position ergonomics	17
higher-speed boat handling	125–128
chartplotter 'lag'	128
contouring waves	126
GNSS 'lag'	128
heeling into wind	127
riding from crest to crest	127
safety of crew and passengers	128
trim	125, 127
hull design and strength	11–12

I

Identification System, Automatic	*see* AIS
IMO (International Maritime Organisation)	8
impellers	19
IRPCS (International Regulations for Preventing Collisions at Sea)	*see* collision regulations

Index

J

jet drives	13, 123
boat handling with	26–28
going astern	27
moving sideways ('crabbing')	28
static	27–28
joystick control systems	14, 29

L

land breeze	87
latitude	67–68
leeway	63
licensing requirements	17–18
lifejackets	93, 116
liferafts	94, 106
lifesaving equipment	93–94
boat	94, 135
liferafts	94, 106
personal	93, 116, 135
lifesaving signals	9, 95
lights, buoyage	54
and position fixing	59
lights, navigation	43–46
locator beacons, personal	93, 135
longitude	67–68

M

maintenance	19–20 see also emergency situations
man overboard (MOB)	89–92 see also searching and search patterns
casualty recovery and aftercare	92
causes	89
chartplotter button	64, 89, 90
dealing with	90–92
Method 1 – into wind	90–91
Method 2 – beam-on approach	91
Williamson Turn	92
preparing for	89
prevention	89
manoeuvring in marinas	30–34
berth, approaching	33–34
berth, leaving	30–32
escape room	32
using lines to assist	31–32, 34
MARPA (Mini Automatic Radar Plotting Aid)	80
MARPOL (International Convention for the Prevention of Pollution from Ships)	8, 9
MCA (Maritime & Coastguard Agency)	17
mooring lines and manoeuvring in marinas	31–32, 34
MRCCs (Maritime Rescue Co-ordination Centres)	95, 96

N

navigation	48–77
buoyage light characteristics	54
chart datums, horizontal	68
chartplotters	see chartplotters
charts	see charts
chartwork symbols	63
'Course to Steer', calculating	61–62
over more than one hour	62
deviation	71
effect of stream on passage	60–62
effect of wind on passage	63
higher-speed	66
latitude and longitude	67–68
leeway	63
passage planning	see passage planning
position, estimating	59–60, 62
position fixing	see position fixing
and radar	80
tides	see tides
tools	65, 69, 70, 71
variation	71
navigator/helm position ergonomics	17

O

outboard engines	12
boat handling with	23, 24–25
twin, leverage with	23
outdrives ('sterndrives')	13, 24–25

P

passage planning	9, 48, 49–50, 135
factors to consider	49
open-water	55
pilotage plan	50–51
pilotage techniques	see pilotage techniques
routes	55
waypoints	55–56
proximity	56
passenger protection	7, 15–16, 124, 128
personal equipment	93, 135
phones, mobile	93
pilotage plans	50–51, 135
pilotage techniques	51–53
back bearing	52

Index

bearing and distance	52
clearing lines and bearings	52
contour lines	53
cross bearings	53
depth lines	53
head bearing	52
and radar	53
speed/time/distance	53
transits	51
turn points	53
pivot points	22, 30
planning, passage	see passage planning
position, estimating	59–60, 62
position fixing	56–59
bearings	57
compass rose waypoint	58, 65
radar	57
using lights at night	59
visually	56
waypoint ladder	58
waypoint web	57, 65
propellers, changing and removing, while afloat	20
'propwalk'	22, 25

Q

qualifications	8, 9

R

radar	78–81
antenna	78
and collision avoidance	80
display	78, 79
MARPA (Mini Automatic Radar Plotting Aid)	80
and navigation	80
and pilotage techniques	53
and position fixing	57
and restricted visibility	42
SARTs (Search and Rescue Transponders)	94
tuning	79–80
radar reflectors	9, 81
radios, handheld VHF	93, 135
regulations	8–9
rescue by helicopter	see helicopter rescue
responsibilities as skipper	6, 8, 9, 16
RIBs (Rigid Inflatable Boats)	15, 16, 89
rougher water, boat handling in	115–124
bars	124
broaching	120
considerations before voyage	115
craft design	124
inlets	124
'pendulum effect'	118
power on or off?	123
power v. speed	123
preparation	116
rolling, resonant	124
safety of crew and passengers	124
sea, types of	see sea, types of
sea anchor	124
'stuffing'	119, 121
swell	123
ventilation	123
water, aerated	123
waves, dealing with	122

S

safety briefings	6, 7, 116
safety equipment	93, 94, 135
safety of crew and passengers	124, 128
sailing craft and collision regulations	40–41, 43
sea, types of	116–122
beam sea	121–122
following sea ('down sea')	119–121
head sea ('up sea')	116–118
sea anchor	124
sea breeze	86
sea fog (advection fog)	85
sea state	114
searching and search patterns	95–101
area searches	96, 97
area v. datum searches	96
and chartplotters	97, 101
Creeping Line Ahead Search	97
datum searches	96, 98–99
datum v. area searches	96
Expanding Square Search	98
'Goalkeeper' Type Search	100
and GNSS	97, 101
multiple vessel search	100
Parallel Track Search	97
sector search	99
sweep width	97
tips for undertaking	101
track spacing	97
seating arrangements	16
shaftdrives	13, 25–26
shapes, day	43, 44–45, 46
shock-mitigation solutions	16
skipper, responsibilities as	6, 8, 9, 16
skipper, role of	6–7
SOLAS (International Convention	8, 9

Index

for the Safety of Life at Sea)
    Chapter V   9, 49, 81, 95
    ('Safety of Navigation')
sound signals   42, 47, 85
spares   20, 135 *see also* emergency situations
speed v. time v. distance   66
stability   108–109
    free surface effect   109
STCW (International Convention on Standards of Training, Certification and Watchkeeping for Seafarers)   8
'sterndrives'   *see* outdrives
stream   *see* tidal streams

T

throttles   14
thrusters   25, 29
tidal heights   *see* tides
tidal streams   75–77
    and boat handling   22
    effect of, on passage   60–62
    and 'tidal hour'   77
    wind against   112–113
tides (tidal heights)   72–75 *see also* tidal streams
    causes   72
    information available   72, 74, 76
    ports, secondary   72, 74–75
    rule of twelfths   73
    spring   73, 75
    terminology   73
    and weather   72
time v. distance v. speed   66
tools   20, 135
torches   65, 93
towing   131–133
    alongside ('side') tow   132
    considerations   133
    long tow   131, 132
    tips for   132–133
    towline length, varying   132–133
Traffic Separation Schemes (TSS)   41
training plan   6
transfers between moving craft   129–130
transits   37, 51
trim   35, 116, 119, 125, 127

U

UNCLOS (United Nations Convention on the Law of the Sea)   8

V

variation   71
VHF radios, handheld   93, 135
visibility, restricted   42, 47, 85

W

wave theory   110–114
    breaking waves   111–112, 122
    localised conditions   113
    sea state   114
    tide-generated waves   112
    wave action   110–111, 122
    wave sources   110
    wave terminology   110, 111, 122
    wind against stream   112–113
    wind direction, change in   113
waves, dealing with   122
waypoint ladder   58
waypoint web   57, 65
waypoints   55–56
    compass rose   58, 65
    proximity   56
weather   82–87 *see also* weather forecasts
    anticyclone (high), passage of   84
    cloud types   85
    and cruising   135
    depression (low), passage of   84
    effects influenced by land   86–87
    fog   42, 47, 85
    fronts, passage of   84, 85
    sea breeze   86
    synoptic charts   86
    wind, katabatic   87
    wind scale, Beaufort   85
weather forecasts   82–83, 86
    general synopsis   83
WGS84 (World Geodetic System 1984) datum   68
wheelhouses   14, 15
Williamson Turn   92
wind, effect of, on passage   63
wind, katabatic   87
wind against stream   112–113
wind scale, Beaufort   85
'windage'   21
working commercially   8–9